THE PATH OF COSMIC CONSCIOUSNESS

A PRACTICAL GUIDE TO HIGHER DIMENSIONS OF REALITY

Other Books in this Series:
The Mystical Philosophy of Jeff Carreira

The Soul of a New Self: Embracing the Future of Being Human
by Jeff Carreira.

Paradigm Shifting: Guiding Evolution from the Inside
by Jeff Carreira.

Higher Self Expression: How to Become an Artist of Possibility
by Jeff Carreira.

The Path of Spiritual Breakthrough: From Awakening to Cosmic Awareness by Jeff Carreira.

Free Resources from Jeff Carreira

Life Without Fear: Meditation as an Antidote to Anxiety
with Jeff Carreira. Visit lifewithoutfear.online

Secrets of Profound Meditation: Six Spiritual Insights that will Transform Your Life with Jeff Carreira.
Visit secretsofprofoundmeditation.com

Foundations of a New Paradigm: A 6-part program designed to shift the way you experience everything with Jeff Carreira.
Visit foundationsofanewparadigm.com

THE PATH OF COSMIC CONSCIOUSNESS

A PRACTICAL GUIDE TO HIGHER DIMENSIONS OF REALITY

JEFF CARREIRA

EMERGENCE EDUCATION
Philadelphia, Pennsylvania

Copyright © 2022 by Jeff Carreira

All rights reserved. Except as permitted under U.S. Copyright Act of 1976, no part of this publication may be reproduced, distributed, or transmitted in any form or by any means, or stored in a database or retrieval system, without the prior written permission of the publisher.

ISBN: 978-1-954642-26-3

Emergence Education
P.O. Box 63767
Philadelphia, PA 19147
EmergenceEducation.com

Interior design by Sophie Peirce.

Printed in the United States of America.

"Art in its highest manifestations is a path to Cosmic Consciousness."

— P.D. Ouspensky

Contents

Introduction ix

Chapter One: A Journey To Your Source 1

Chapter Two: The Field of Awareness 9

Chapter Three: The Invention of an Idea 21

Chapter Four: Poets, Gurus and Spiritual Transmission 35

Chapter Five: The Evolution of Consciousness 57

Chapter Six: The Awakening of the Cosmos 83

Chapter Seven: The Fourth-Dimension and Creative Illumination 107

Chapter Eight: Essentials of Spiritual Attunement 137

Chapter Nine: A Life of Cosmic Prayer 167

   Selected Bibliography 177

   About the Author 179

Jeff Carreira

Introduction

IN THE YEARS JUST PRIOR to writing this book I have experienced a deepening recognition of how central the experience of cosmic consciousness is to my spiritual life. This is not an entirely new revelation, but it is a deeper recognition that experiencing, living, and sharing cosmic consciousness is the reason for my existence. It is my purpose. It is the opening I was born for. I don't want to make this sound like I am in some way a perfect representation of that high ideal. I am not. I am on the path. I have been on the path for a long time. I have had many profound experiences and have attained some stability in a higher perspective, but I am still on the path. What I can say is that I remain as committed and enthusiastic about that path today as I was thirty years ago when I started out.

The phrase *cosmic consciousness* is wonderfully vivid in naming what is undoubtedly one of the highest forms of spiritual experience. In this book we will explore not only the experience of cosmic consciousness, but also its manifestation as a transformed experience of human life. We will call this transformed life, *universal being*, and for our purposes I want to ask you to think about *universal being* as simply the living manifestation of cosmic consciousness. This miraculous possibility exists within all of us and in these pages I will share everything I know about how it can be attained.

It is important to make clear right at the start that this is not an academic analysis of the subject. Although there is a great deal of wisdom in this book about cosmic consciousness and universal being, I did not write it just to impart information. The main reason for writing this book is to provide a practical guide for those who want to experience and embody cosmic consciousness through the transformation of their own life.

It is my firm conviction that many of us, and perhaps all of us, can open our awareness to the magnificent view of cosmic consciousness. In addition, through specific forms of spiritual work, I also believe we can transform our lives to become a profound expression of that higher awareness. This possibility is available to anyone, yet there is no shortcut to universal being. There is no way to avoid the work that it will take to liberate yourself from your current identity and be reborn into a new one. There are, and have always been, those rare cases when an unsought for sudden realization resulted in a dramatic transformation, but these cases are few and far between. Your chances of winning a million dollar lottery are probably better than attaining enlightenment spontaneously in this way.

For most of us the path requires diligent effort and perseverance. And even with the most intensive effort and perseverance there is always an element of grace or karma involved. Spiritual realization always arrives mysteriously in the end. Regardless of the amount of practice or study we have done, the final dawning of insight comes as a surprise. We can say that our efforts made us available for the mystery of realization, but it did not cause it. If we are fortunate enough to make direct contact with the unknowable source of higher love and wisdom, it can only be thought of as a gift of the divine, or as the fruition of our karma, but either way the ultimate source is mysterious.

This book explores the reality of both cosmic consciousness and universal being as well as the attitudes, practices and contemplations that create the optimal conditions for realizing them. Because the source of this blessing is a mystery, it is best not to think of achieving or attaining this miracle but instead to think in terms of inviting it into your awareness and into your life. In this book we will envision how to make this invitation in the most attractive way possible to maximize the chances that a miracle will occur in your life and divinity will bestow her gift upon you.

This book will be especially useful for those who sincerely aspire to, and feel ready for, the experience of cosmic consciousness and a higher life of universal being. It is also well suited for those who may not feel ready or willing to transform their life right now, but who aspire to live on a higher plane of being one day. If you have tasted a higher possibility for human life and aspire to live it, I hope to provide you with a roadmap to get there and guidance for traversing the terrain ahead.

CHAPTER ONE

A Journey To Your Source

"That which you are seeking is causing you to seek."

- Zen Saying

Jeff Carreira

HERE I AM AT THE start of writing this book, asking myself, does the world really need another book about cosmic consciousness? Probably not, but I need to write it, and I know that some people will need to read exactly the book I am about to write. At least I believe they will. And so I'm writing it in part for all of the people, and I see you as one of them, that I believe will benefit from reading it.

The reason I think you might benefit from this book is because I assume you decided to read it because you want to discover and experience cosmic consciousness yourself. I don't intend to write a book *about* cosmic consciousness - partly because books like that already exist and many of them are excellent - but also because my interest is not in understanding the phenomenon. Rather, I feel compelled by the possibility of experiencing and ultimately living the miracle of it.

I want this book to be a practical guide to cosmic consciousness. That means that it will give you perspectives to explore and ideas to contemplate that will ignite a dramatic shift in your state of consciousness and ultimately in your way of living. I will share some theoretical understanding and historical background, but all of it will be in service of enhancing your capacity to make use of the guidance offered. Fundamentally this book was born out of my own experience, which is ultimately all any of us have to share. If this book is successful, you will be able to use it to shape practices and inquiry that will carry you into a vast and utterly profound view of reality. If a shift in consciousness of this magnitude is what you want, then I believe you will find this book very helpful.

However, I am not just writing this book for you. Like any author, I'm also writing it for myself. I have experienced cosmic consciousness, or at least something that fits the descriptions of cosmic consciousness that I've read about, and that experience dramatically impacted the course of my life. It happened during a long silent meditation retreat. I was sitting in meditation when I suddenly found myself floating up in the air. Then I realized that I wasn't floating upward, I was expanding. I was still sitting cross legged on the floor but my body was growing and my head was moving upward. My line of vision passed through the roof of the building and up into the sky until I could see for miles around me. Slowly I climbed higher as my body grew larger and larger. Soon I could see the curve of Earth beneath me as my body completely engulfed the world. And still I continued to grow. Eventually the entire solar system was inside me and as I continued on this magnificent journey of expansion I lost sight of the Earth and the Sun. There was an ocean of stars inside my body now and slowly I began to stop growing.

My body had extended to the furthest edges of the universe and I knew the entire cosmos was my body. I was a cosmic being. I realized that I was home. I felt a tremendous sense of love pouring through me. This was where I belonged. I relaxed and rested in that exquisite state for a short time and then I began to shrink again. I was not afraid. I was ready. My journey of expansion reversed until I was sitting again on the floor in my familiar body. I was back in my human form and I remembered that this was not the first trip I had taken to the outer reaches of the cosmos. I distinctly remembered, although I had forgotten until then, that as a small child I would regularly venture into my cosmic source by staring into my own eyes in a mirror. I remembered very clearly the day I stared into my own eyes and was dismayed to realize that I couldn't do it anymore. I had become stranded on Earth and I was going to have to find a way to get along here without access to my cosmic being. It was a very sad day.

Somehow I managed to forget those frequent trips to my cosmic self, but now that I had remembered them again I could see clearly that my entire spiritual search had begun with those early adventures beyond the world. My lifelong interest and obsession with spirituality was a direct result of those early experiences. This book is emerging out of me now because recently I have felt called home, back to the omnipresent and primordial source of my being. I hear her calling me like a melody barely audible in the distance. She invites me to return, not just to experience her again, but to rest with her and live by her side. In this book one of the things that we will discuss is the use of cosmic prayers as a means of attracting cosmic consciousness into our lives. Writing this book and the research, study and contemplation that it requires, is all part of my cosmic prayer.

I see this book as an extension of and expansion upon my earlier book, *The Path of Spiritual Breakthrough*. In that book I outlined the co-creative nature of spiritual growth by examining some of my own spiritual breakthroughs. This book is specifically targeted at the breakthrough into cosmic consciousness and the exploration you will find in these pages is aimed at guiding you into that breakthrough.

Since you are here reading this book, I can only assume that you are already awake to the possibility and profound potential of cosmic consciousness. You may object saying that you want to have that realization, but you haven't had it yet. I would contend that you have had it, at least once, in this lifetime or some other, even though you may not remember having had it. I say this with confidence because my experience tells me that interest in cosmic consciousness only appears in those who have at least tasted it already. Without at least a taste of cosmic consciousness, this book would appear to you as words about nothing. But that is not how they appeared to you. They appeared to you as words about something, and specifically something that you felt drawn toward now and probably have been for a while. You are awake to the possibility. To me that means that somewhere in your past, whether you remember it or not, a door opened for you. You may have walked a long way from that opening without giving it any thought, but it is there, and it is calling you to read this book now.

Stop for a moment and focus on your interest in reading this book. What caused you to buy it, to pick it up, and to be reading it now? Can you find it? Can you see the energy that compelled you? Sit for a moment and be with the interest that brought you here. Where did it come from? Maybe you can see a history to it. Maybe you read another book that led you to this one, or you have a friend who ignited your interest by talking with you about matters of higher consciousness. You might be an ardent seeker who has engaged with spiritual practices for years. You might have spent time with teachers or visiting holy places around the world. Of course, you might also think of yourself as someone without spiritual inclinations at all and have no idea why you were compelled.

None of that matters, look at the interest itself, the energy that compelled you to be reading now. If you could trace it back through all of your personal spiritual history, and beyond that through the spiritual experiences you've had but were never consciously aware of, and perhaps even to spiritual histories and experiences you had in lifetimes you lived before this one, if you trace that interest all the way back, somewhere it will be the result of some direct taste, large or small, of cosmic consciousness. There is a Zen saying that states, "That which you are seeking is causing you to seek." And so it is.

I suggest that as you read this book, you periodically return to this simple little exercise. Bring your attention back to the interest that brought you to this book. Everything you need is in the energy that brought you here. If this book has any spiritual power in it then it will stoke the flames of the intention that brought you here and provide a clearer path to follow back to your original encounter with cosmic consciousness. Typically we will think of that encounter as something that happened in the past, but it never is. That encounter is happening right now, and the interest you feel is the distant melody of it, barely audible, calling you home. This is a journey to your source. Not a source that exists in the past, but the source that you are emerging out of right now.

SUMMARY OF EXERCISES

Stop for a moment and focus on your interest in reading this book. What caused you to buy it, to pick it up, and to be reading it now? Can you find it? Can you see the energy that compelled you? Sit for a moment and be with the interest that brought you here.

Describe in a notebook or journal about what you see in this investigation.

Chapter Two

The Field of Awareness

*""The limits of my language are the limits of my mind.
All I know is what I have words for."*

- Ludwig Wittgenstein

Jeff Carreira

Now it is time to start our journey and the first question to answer is, what is cosmic consciousness? This is a very easy question to answer. Cosmic consciousness is a phrase in the English language. That's all it is. It is a phrase consisting of two words, *cosmic* and *consciousness*. Of course, that answer, although entirely correct, is hardly satisfying because it immediately begs a bigger question; what does the phrase cosmic consciousness mean? It may seem like a useless step in answering the question to even mention that it is a linguistic term, after all we all already know that. We do of course know that, but in fact we often forget, and when we do we assume that the phrase itself is something, then we remember that it is a mere phrase. A tree is not the word that represents it, just like I am not my name.

It is easy for us to be lazy and assume that if we know the words that describe something then we know it itself, but that is not necessarily so, and thinking that it is will keep us from journeying beyond the words to the reality of what we seek. This book, so full of words, is not about the words, it is about the reality that the words (hopefully) point to. As I intend to take you through the very subtle territory of spiritual exploration in as simple, clear and thorough a way as I can, we cannot gloss over the fact that the phrase cosmic consciousness is just words. If we ignore this obvious fact it would be easy to immediately go on to define cosmic consciousness using other words. If the words were well chosen and articulated to define the phrase, it would feel satisfying to your intellect. You might believe that you understood what cosmic consciousness is, but you would be no closer to actually being what it is.

If we are going to go into such a delicate and subtle exploration carefully we need to start out with a mutual understanding of the difference between understanding and true knowing. This is an understanding that I am suggesting we will need to carry with us for the remainder of this book. I am not sharing this distinction because it is right, although it may be. In fact, I am not sharing anything in this book because it is right. The domain of right vs. wrong is the domain of understanding, and although I will share some understanding with you, ultimately what I want to share is true knowledge. You could use the word wisdom in exchange for knowledge, but that feels a bit presumptuous. I want to share knowledge which we can define as the immediate knowing that comes from direct experience. To illustrate with an example we could imagine that someone read a book about the city of Lisbon and understood what they read, but that is different from the person who visits Lisbon, walks its streets and speaks with the people there. The second person knows Lisbon, the first only understands some things about it.

But let's back up and move slowly. We are making a distinction between understanding and knowing in much the same way that the romantic poet Samual Taylor Coleridge did in his magnum opus text *Aids to Reflection*. Understanding for Coleridge is linguistic in nature. When we understand something we understand it in words. We can describe it and explain it. To say it more technically, understanding is something that happens in symbols that are used as signs for real things. The problem is that the symbols we use to signify real things are not the things they signify. A sign that says "restaurant" is not a place where you can eat. The sign stands for the place where you can eat. To understand or experience something implies that you know what the words in the sign stand for in reality.

We use words to stand for real things. They hold meaning

metaphorically, but at the risk of belaboring the point, the words are not the things they stand for. They are just words that signify the actual thing. But we often confuse words with reality. We assume that our words point unerringly to real things. For simple things this may be a safe assumption. As the things we want to represent in words become more complex and subtle, the words we have to describe them with, quickly prove to be woefully inadequate to the task.

It is very difficult to come to a mutual agreement on the understanding of a phrase as complex and subtle as cosmic consciousness, but it is not impossible. In the name of moving very slowly into these muddy waters, let's consider what it means to come to an understanding about anything.

The brilliant twentieth century philosopher Ludwig Wittgenstein spoke about understanding in terms of word games. If you strip it down to the bone, what it really means to understand has to do with sentences and how they correspond with each other. Saying that we understand something means that there will be a predictable congruence between the words and actions of different speakers. Imagine that I say to a small child, what is that? And she says in response, it is a cat. If I understood that the thing I pointed to when I asked the question was a cat, then I would see that the child and I had the same understanding. Understanding really means that we are using the same words to signify some aspect of reality. Again, for understanding something as simple as what a cat is, this seldom poses any problems, and because we don't generally run into problems we get lazy about how we understand understanding. We end up assuming that congruence in sentences proves mutual understanding and that every time two people can speak using words that seem to correspond in meaning they must be understanding the same thing by those words.

In our laziness, we say, *this is a cat*, when what we really mean is *this is a thing that I signify with the word cat*. The artist René

Margitte made this point graphically clear in a painting depicting a pipe that had the words, this is not a pipe, written under it. The painting was a representation of a pipe just like the word pipe is a representation of a pipe, but neither the painting nor the word is an actual pipe. Unfortunately for convenience sake we forget that we speak in signs and assume that we are exchanging realities, as I have already stated, for so many of the things we would speak about that works very well.

Remember, understanding is determined by success in the word game called language. In the simple word game of our example above, the question *what is this?* is followed by the answer, *it's a cat*. The game is over and whoever gave the answer has won and is acknowledged as being someone who understands. If the answer, *it is a toaster* were given there would be a disruption in the game. Whoever asked the question would receive an answer that does not match their understanding and so they would conclude the other does not understand and a mutual understanding would need to be established before further conversation could continue.

You may be wondering why I am making such a big deal out of something so trivial. The reason begins to become clear if we consider the possibility that the child had been taught that the furry creature we know as a cat, was called a toaster. Their answer, *it is a toaster*, would then be accurate to their understanding, but different from ours. Who is right? There is no necessary link that connects a word to an object in reality. What is right or wrong is determined by consensus. If our understanding matches the majority understanding it is considered right. If it differs, it is wrong.

Understanding is a way of representing things and ideas in words so that they can be passed on to other people. In order to share ideas this way we must do it according to the rules of language and our success in being able to follow the rules of languages is what demonstrates our understanding. Using our simple example again, there is a rule that demands that when I am asked what that furry creature is, that I respond with the word cat. If I respond with another word then I have broken the rule and proven that I do not understand.

I could probably, and to some extent I will, take you through a long language game around the question, what is cosmic consciousness? If I play the game well, I will teach you rules for using language that will help us come to a mutual understanding of what cosmic consciousness is. Once we have both learned the rules we will be able to speak for hours about this profound topic without ever encountering a disruption in our use of language. We will both have the same understanding of cosmic consciousness, but cosmic consciousness is not an object that can easily be pointed to, so how do we know that what I am talking about as cosmic consciousness is the same as what you are talking about even if we are using the same words? Here is where we feel the limits of words.

The phrase cosmic consciousness doesn't, nor do any other words we could use to describe it, necessarily tell us anything about what cosmic consciousness is. We can get very good at speaking about cosmic consciousness without ever having experienced it. We can know all about it, and even speak about it for hours without having any actual experience of it. Understanding simply tells us how well we can use words in the game of language, and you can get very good at that without having any direct experience of what you are talking about.

We see this all the time. People can learn about anything from other people or from books. If they study hard they can become an expert on a topic. Imagine someone who spends years studying about a far away country. They can become quite an expert on the geography, laws, food and customs of that country without ever having visited. Most people who had not visited the country for themselves would be very impressed, but someone who grew up in that country would undoubtedly be able to tell that this person had never had any direct experience..

What I want to share with you is true knowledge not understanding. I want you to experience cosmic consciousness for yourself. The reality of cosmic consciousness can never be contained in words, alas, words are what I have to share with, so I am offering a cautionary note here at the start of this book. You can read this book and understand the words and you can even get good at speaking about cosmic consciousness, but if that is as far as the book takes you I will have failed in my purpose. I want you to experience this miracle - to truly know it, not just understand it. In order for me to be successful in this I will need your help. In order to experience cosmic consciousness for yourself you will need to do more than read this book, you will need to work with it. Do the exercises that I suggest, think about the questions that I raise. There is no way that I can guarantee that your perception will open to your own cosmic being, but what I do know is that it definitely might.

When Coleridge made a distinction between understanding and knowing (he actually used the word reason rather than knowing, but I find that confusing) I believe he was making a distinction between knowing about things in the way that is contained in language, and the knowing of things directly. Coleridge had a particularly beautiful and intriguing way of describing the nature of reason. He used phrases like a "seeing light" and talked about an "enlightening eye" that contains "a power that sees by its own light." He also uses the phrase "universal light" in his descriptions of our capacity for direct knowing and I believe that cosmic consciousness is direct contact with exactly the universal seeing light that he described.

Understanding happens in our minds. It happens in that part of our awareness that sees and manipulates words and places them into meaningful order. We could call this our rational or logical mind if we want, although that should not imply that the other form of knowing is irrational or illogical.

Direct knowing does not happen in our minds in any localized sense. It happens everywhere. For Coleridge and other romantic thinkers, reality was not an unconscious expanse of space, reality was a conscious field. Anything that arose in that field was immediately known, and here we would be better to think in terms of the ancient word gnosis, a deep and direct knowing of things. This is not a form of knowing that is deduced or derived through logic. It is an immediate perception. You could say an intuition. Beyond our rational linguistic minds we are all part of a field of knowing and if we can bring our awareness there we gain access to the direct knowing of things. I believe that in the deepest reaches of this field we find the immediate spiritual knowing that the ancients referred to. This is where I believe we will find cosmic consciousness.

The first part of our exploration has led us to an understanding that cosmic consciousness is something like a field of conscious knowing, but we do not want to settle for this vague understanding. This book is a practical guide to cosmic consciousness and so I want to give you a way to practice based on this understanding in service of leading you into a direct recognition of it.

Take a moment to sit quietly and look around you. Perhaps you are sitting in a room filled with objects like I am. In front of me is a computer, against the wall to my right is a bookcase full of books. I can see trees blowing in the breeze outside. Sit quietly and pay attention to the things you see and hear around you. Notice how you relate to all of those sights and sounds. Generally we think of the bookcase as existing over there against the wall and the sight of it existing inside of us. We imagine the trees to be outside the window, but we experience the sound of them inside our heads.

See if you can find that relationship to the things around you. Now think differently. Imagine that the bookcase exists over there against the wall, but your vision of it exists there too. Imagine that your eyes are not taking in the site and delivering it to your brain to process, think of it as being visible over there where it is. It exists in a field of conscious awareness. It is not entering you so that you become aware of it, it is being experienced exactly where it is. Do the same for the sound of the trees, maybe they are heard right there where they are. Maybe the whole world is being experienced all around you right where it is, not in your head, but in a vast ever present field of awareness.

I know this is not the way we are trained to experience, but try it anyway. I am not asking you to do this because it is right, I just want you to experience a new sensibility. We are trained to see ourselves as a conscious thing in the universe. Everything else is just sitting out there and we perceive it in our heads. Try perceiving a different way. Allow the whole world to be alive and consciously aware right where it is. Everything is created from the "seeing light" of cosmic consciousness. Don't worry if you find this difficult we will continue to return to this shift again and again, but do keep trying. Give yourself some time everyday to practice this flip in perspective.

Imagine that everything in the world around you is conscious and alive right there where it is. Yes from our human perspective we experience everything from over here where we are, but how does the cosmos experience everything? The cosmos is everything. The cosmos doesn't exist separate from everything. To the cosmos everything arises as an experience, not as an object to be experienced later. Try the experiment. It's difficult, but that is to be expected. If we long to shift into a cosmic perspective, if we aspire to attain cosmic consciousness, we will need to stretch the perceptual powers of our minds. New possibilities of perception don't just appear to us, we need to extend ourselves into them. I call these exercises of perceptual extension the practice of creative illumination. We must engage in the creative act of illuminating new possibilities in our own experience. Exercises like this will be included at the end of every chapter of this book. Please work with them. Don't assume they will be hard, but don't stop if they are. Just do them as often as you can. This is one of the most powerful ways that I know of to move toward and ultimately into cosmic consciousness.

SUMMARY OF EXERCISES

Take a moment to sit quietly and look around you. Notice how you relate to all of those sights and sounds as existing out there away from you while we locate the sensation of those things as if they are inside of us. We imagine that the world is outside, but we experience it inside our heads. Can you experience as if your experience of the things around you is happening not in your head, but right there exactly where they are located. Imagine that everything in the world around you is conscious and alive right there where it is.

Describe in a notebook or journal about what you see in this investigation.

CHAPTER THREE

The Invention of an Idea

"...though the world does not change with a change of paradigm, the scientist afterward works in a different world."

- Thomas S. Kuhn

I WANT THIS BOOK TO generate a momentum that will lead to your own awakening to cosmic consciousness and the best way I can do that is to help you fall in love with not only the idea of it, but more importantly the possibility of it. If you aspire to cosmic consciousness you have to be in love with it. When we love something we give it our attention, we want to hold it close, we take care of it, cherish it, and become sensitive to it. This is exactly what I want for you. One of the ways to help you fall in love with the idea of cosmic consciousness is to tell you about the history of it. The story around this particular terminology is a romantic one full of poetry, passion, adventure, mysticism, and perseverance. It is always valuable to trace the origin of an idea because the sentiments of the originators of that idea become part of the idea and although we may long have forgotten who it was who first thought it, the idea itself will always contain a little part of them.

The idea referred to as cosmic consciousness was probably most powerfully brought into public attention with the publication of William James' magnum opus, *The Varieties of Religious Experience* in 1902. The book was an immediate bestseller and doubtlessly introduced many readers to the new and wonderful conception of cosmic consciousness. In his text on religious experience James quotes extensively from another book published just one year earlier, Dr. Richard Maurice Bucke's *Cosmic Consciousness*. The extensive referencing of Bucke's book in *The Varieties of Religious Experience* surely helped build a larger audience for it. James' first mention of cosmic consciousness is in relation to the use of Walt Whitman as an example of the healthy minded personality type. This type is born with an innate attitude toward wholeness and goodness. They are existential optimists you could say who are prone to seeing the interconnected wholeness of things. Whitman is held up as a prime example of this type of spiritual disposition in James' book. Whitman also figures prominently in Bucke's book as the person who most perfectly embodies cosmic consciousness in modern times.

James and many others credit Bucke with the term cosmic consciousness and it is certainly true that the Canadian born physician did introduce the term, with James' support, to a wide audience of seekers. But Bucke himself does not take credit for inventing the term. Instead he admits that he learned the phrase from his friend Edward Carpenter who had first used the term in his 1892 travelog of journeys through India and Ceylon (present day Sri Lanka) *From Adam's Peak to Elephanta*. Four chapters of Edward's book are devoted to reporting on a two month period he spent in the city of Columbo under the tutelage of Ramaswamy, an adept of the south Indian school of Hinduism.

In these remarkable four chapters Edwards outlines the basic principles of the path to enlightenment that he learned from his teacher. In all humility Edwards admits that he cannot do justice to a full and exact explication of the teachings he received, instead he claims only to share in his own words and using modern language the essence of what he discovered about how a person can be lifted into a supernatural region of consciousness. He states that the higher order of consciousness to which Hindu mysticism aspires can be called universal or cosmic consciousness. He admits that he does not know of the exact equivalent of this phrase in Hindu philosophy, but he feels that it is a good phrase to capture the essential meaning of the Hindu term *Sat-Chit-Ananda*, which can literally be translated as *Existence-Consciousness-Bliss* and is used in the East to denote the most essential experience of being. The unchanging eternal and infinite source of being in the Hindu tradition is known as Brahman. So Sat-Chit-Ananda can be thought of as the felt experience of Brahman and sometimes these two terms are used almost interchangeably because the experience cannot ultimately be separated from the fact.

The term cosmic consciousness began as a translation into modern English of the ancient Vedantic idea of Sat-Chit-Ananda or Brahman and so our pursuit of this miraculous state of being must include some exploration of the ancient tradition from which it was derived. Here again we run into the problem of language. Is the idea of cosmic consciousness equivalent to the idea of Sat-Chit-Ananda or Brahman? The way that we commonly think of language would tell us that it must be, because as we have already discussed, we are taught to see language merely as a pointer that directs us toward real things that exist independent of the words we use to describe them. Juliet in the famous Shakespeare play announces that, "A rose by any other name would smell as sweet." With this phrase she asserts that there is nothing in a name that changes what it names. In other words, what we call something has no effect on what it is. This is the popular modern attitude toward language, but I want to suggest that it is not the most useful attitude to adopt in our explorations of higher consciousness.

There were times and cultures in which words were not seen as passive markers that merely pointed toward the real things underneath them. Words were considered magical and the act of naming something was felt to create what it named as much as identify it. Words, and the naming of things, was recognized to have a creative power, and this attitude is the one I suggest we adopt for our current exploration. The idea that the language we use might be intimately and co-creatively linked to the reality we experience is an essential contemplation for those of us who are seeking to become a vessel for cosmic being. The reason words are so important on our spiritual journey is because words have the power to open up new worlds of possibility to us, and the objective of our spiritual pursuits is to discover new worlds of possibility.

In his monumental book *The Structures of Scientific Revolutions*, Princeton University professor Thomas Kuhn makes this point using the example of the scientific discovery of oxygen. From the times of Aristotle until well into the second half of the sixteenth century, air was assumed to be a single gas. In 1775 the scientist Joseph Priestley had developed a means of cleaning air of phlogiston. Phlogiston was the substance contained in air that was imagined to be responsible for combustion. Things burned when they were in contact with a significant amount of phlogiston. Priestley believed that he had stripped air of phlogiston and created dephlogisticated air.

Another scientist, Antoine Lavoisier, a decade younger and perhaps more radical in his thinking, didn't believe in the phlogiston theory of combustion. He repeated Priestley's method and obtained the same resultant gas, but he didn't believe that he was seeing clean air, he thought that he had separated out a component gas of air that he called oxygen.

The question Kuhn raises is, who discovered oxygen. Did Priestley discover it even though he thought it was dephlogisticated air? Or did Lavoisier discover it when he obtained the same result and identified it as an independent gas called oxygen. This debate has continued without an answer for over two hundred years. Using the logic of a rose by any other name, we might say that Priestley discovered oxygen even though he misidentified it, but generally history has favored Lavoisier as having made the discovery of oxygen because he correctly identified it, correctly at least to our current understanding of the substance.

This is an interesting point. Did Lavoisier identify oxygen correctly? What does that even mean? It is possible, and arguably likely, that our ideas about what oxygen is, will be different and perhaps radically different in the future. At that point Lavoisier will be downgraded from the stature of the person who had correctly identified oxygen to just another scientist who had tried and failed to discover the truth. It might be more useful to say that Lavoisier invented the idea of oxygen, rather than that he discovered a gas.

What is most interesting about the invention of oxygen is not the potential fact that Lavoisier had correctly identified a real substance. What is most interesting is what happened as a result of his articulation of what he discovered as a new substance. Seeing oxygen as a separate gas, meant that air was now seen as a mixture of at least two different gasses. Lavoisier's naming of oxygen helped initiate the scientific revolution that led to the development of modern chemistry. Thomas Kuhn identifies this revolution as a paradigm shift, and describes how it led to a radical change in how chemistry was understood and practiced. The new paradigm opened up a new world of possibility.

Our current paradigm tells us that we live in a material universe that is real. Real means that it exists independent of what we think about it, and that it was there waiting to be discovered before we had any idea about it. When we perceive something new we assume that we are discovering something that was already there. I don't believe this is the most useful way to think, especially in relation to our spiritual pursuits. I believe that we are co-creating reality as much as we are discovering it. When we see something differently we are not just discovering something, we are inventing it. This way of thinking allows us to see that by creating the term cosmic consciousness. Edward Carpenter was creating a new spiritual possibility, even though the new possibility was being created on top of an older one. Cosmic Consciousness was a product of Edward Carpenter's experience and understanding of an Eastern notion of enlightenment, but it was articulated in a new way and a different language and I would argue that the term created an entryway that was more inviting, more intelligible, and more accessible to Western spiritual seekers. I would also generalize this notion, and did so in *The Path of Spiritual Breakthrough*, to say that understanding the co-creative power of how we articulate our spiritual experiences changes how we engage with our spiritual pursuits and dramatically expands what is possible for us.

This shift in perspective, or paradigm shift if you will, was crucial to me on my spiritual path. It was this insight more than another that opened me to a new spiritual world. This is something that I want to be sure to express clearly to you because I know that it can have a dramatic and positive effect on your spiritual life.

The insight hit me, as many of mine do, in meditation. I was sitting at the start of an hour of practice and very quickly I felt a numbness in my toe. In meditation I would ordinarily ignore that feeling in the name of letting everything be as it is. But this time was different. As I began to relax and let go of the feeling, I realized that this was also doing something. I suddenly saw that this numbness had come into my practice for a reason and I decided to surrender to it rather than ignore it. Immediately the numbness expanded until it ran through my entire body. I had been transported into a state of sublime calm. It was as if I was covered in a cocoon of vibrating energetic peacefulness. Meditation was so easy then. I simply sat in a cloud of peace and I wasn't even tempted to struggle with anything that arose in awareness.

I would eventually describe this simple gesture of surrendering to what arises in meditation rather than merely passively witnessing it, as creative illumination. I believe that our spiritual progress is as much a co-creation as it is a discovery. We participate in the unfolding of spirit by selectively surrendering to those inner movements that call us. Everything changed in my spiritual life as a result of this insight. Beforehand, I was constantly wanting to discover something that I assumed existed outside of the experience I was already having, but afterwards, I was simply paying attention to the experience I was already having to see where it wanted to take me. This experience, the one you are having right now, is the one you've been waiting for. This moment is already the moment of the spirit's emergence into being. The subtle energies of our inner being are always calling to us, inviting us to merge with them and surrender to them so that they can manifest through us and open up a new world of possibility for us to explore.

Naming and describing these experiences, for ourselves and anyone we talk to about them, is an important part of manifesting them in reality. Words are the tools that we have, as imperfect as they are, to share our inner experiences with others. When we articulate our inner revelations, we invite others to experience them. This is what Edward Carpenter did when he invented the term cosmic consciousness. I propose that Carpenter did not just invent the term, he invented a new spiritual possibility. Yes he was drawing on wisdom from the Vedantic tradition, but he was doing more than translating an idea into a different language, he was interpreting it, re-creating it in a novel way. He was not simply expressing an eastern idea, he was attempting to express his own understanding as a modern Westerner of that idea. He was adding something to the picture. The phrase cosmic consciousness was a novel western articulation for what he had learned that the terms Sat-Chit-Ananda and Brahman referred to in India, and it was more than that. The term was also a new doorway, a new access point to an experience that has been known in India since ancient times. And it might even be more than this. The term might have brought a new experience of that ultimate realization to life and initiated a new world of possibility around it. The question I am asking you to consider is, just how creative are we? How much are we adding and changing reality by articulating our spiritual experiences powerfully? We don't have to assume anything about the co-creative nature of spiritual articulation, but I think it will be very valuable to you if you are willing to be open to the possibility that these articulations are much more creative than you might have imagined before.

It is important for us to explore the Vedantic roots of the term. We need to know what was inspiring Carpenter and those that followed him. We need to feel the beauty and the elegance of that mystical tradition so that we can see how it was brought into a new form. And we need to feel the tremendous power of a spiritual lineage that has been practiced for thousands of years. All of this will help open us to the direct experience of cosmic consciousness, but it will also be important to be receptive to the possibility that cosmic consciousness is a different experience than what was so beautifully described in the Vedas, and even more so, to be open to the further possibility, as I will argue for later, that your experience of cosmic consciousness may be uniquely your own. You may not discover cosmic consciousness, you may invent it for yourself. When you experience the miracle of this higher awareness, it will be because you entered into a creative union with the subtle stirrings of your inner being and co-created an experience of cosmic consciousness.

This co-creative view of spiritual progress flies in the face of our cultural commitment to the orthodox belief in a pre-existing reality. We can't just make this up!, we might complain. Our discoveries must be real, not imaginary! When every scientist in existence believed that air was a single gas, were they wrong? For centuries that understanding fit almost every aspect of their observable world. What would have happened if Lavoisier had not named oxygen as oxygen, or if all of the other scientists of the time had rejected the new conception. Would it be true anyway? What if science and chemistry had developed in a completely different direction so that today we would all commonly believe in the substance known as phlogiston that caused things to burn? Would it be untrue? How many ideas that we believe without question to be true today, will be recognized as false tomorrow?

I believe that the world we live in is as much a world of created beliefs as it is of objective reality. I can exchange the paper in my pocket for a meal because I, and the person I am exchanging it with, both believe that it is money that is worth something. If I end up somewhere that does not share my belief about money, it is reduced to paper. How much of the world that we live in is created by shared beliefs and commitments? Is a table still a table if it is placed in a culture that has no idea what a table is? Did oxygen exist before Lavoisier named it? Was the world always round even when everyone believed it was flat? How deeply creative is reality? That is a question that is at the heart of the idea of cosmic consciousness because the most profound thing that cosmic consciousness reveals is that the universe itself is alive and creative. But is that true even if we don't know it, or do we make it true when we believe it? These are not questions that I can answer. I am not sure if they are questions that can be answered, but I feel strongly that they are questions that must be considered on our journey.

Now it is time to engage in your own contemplation. Please think about a few of your most significant spiritual insights or breakthroughs. If you are like most people you will relate to them as discoveries. You will imagine that through them you experienced something that you had never experienced before and consciously or unconsciously you assumed that what you discovered had always been there waiting for you to find it.

What if it was not there? What if it came into being as you experienced it? Choose one of your transformative realizations and think about it. Try to imagine it as it happened as clearly as you can. Try to remember what you were doing that might have contributed to initiating the shift in awareness, and how you related to the shift that then shaped how it continued to unfold in your life. Think of your life since that time. You will probably think of it as the same life, lived in the same world, but with the addition of a new understanding, a new experience. What did you discover, what did you learn, and how did it shape your life and your world?

Now imagine the possibility that the world you entered after the breakthrough was not the same as the one you lived in before. Imagine that you had stepped through that experience into a new world. You probably assumed that it was the same world, but what if it wasn't? What if you had participated in the creation of a new world that you then inhabited? Do your best to feel your way into this possibility. How does it make you feel? How does it affect your sense of what is possible? Is it empowering? Is it exciting, frightening, or inspiring? Feel your way into this possibility and write about how it feels in a journal.

In order to prepare for a shift as radical as that represented by the leap into cosmic consciousness, we must relax our strict adherence to an assumption of a pre-existing reality. We must embrace a much more fluid relationship to existence so that we have the wiggle room that might allow us to slip into a different world altogether.

SUMMARY OF EXERCISES

Choose one of your transformative realizations and think about it. Try to imagine it as it happened as clearly as you can. What did you discover, what did you learn, and how did it shape your life and your world? Now imagine that the world you entered after the breakthrough was not the same as the one you lived in before. Imagine that when you had that experience you actually had stepped into a new world and have been living there ever since.

Describe in a notebook or journal about what you see in this investigation.

Jeff Carreira

CHAPTER FOUR

Poets, Gurus and Spiritual Transmission

"The truth which poetry expresses takes two forms, the truth of life and the truth of that which works in life, the truth of the inner spirit."

- Sri Aurobindo

Jeff Carreira

IN THE LAST CHAPTER WE explored how ideas and the reality they represent are intimately entwined with the language we use to describe them. In this sense the idea of cosmic consciousness was more than just the discovery of something that already existed. It was an invention, but it was not an invention that emerged out of thin air. It emerged within a context that was both historical and personal. The history of an idea and the people who influenced it as it was being born, become part of the idea. In this chapter we will explore the birth of the idea of cosmic consciousness.

I have already stated briefly that the idea of cosmic consciousness was brought into public prominence through the combined efforts of Richard Maurice Bucke and William James. It will be beneficial to our exploration to look more closely at the person who can rightly be seen as the originator of the phrase, Edward Carpenter.

Edward Carpenter was an English intellectual and lecturer who would become best known as a social reformer and human rights activist. He was also a spiritual seeker, an individual like so many of us, who was compelled to discover life's deeper meaning and significance, and even more so, to live it. In his autobiography, Carpenter said that after ten years of dedication to the attainment of this higher consciousness, what he had realized is that the entire point of spiritual work is the harmonizing of body and soul, outer and inner. This lofty attainment, of lived awakening, he saw as the result of cosmic consciousness.

As I have stated repeatedly, I want this to be a practical guide to cosmic consciousness not merely an intellectual study of the phenomenon. I am assuming that you, like Carpenter, want to experience and live cosmic consciousness and so in this chapter, I will begin to outline what I see as the fundamental path that leads to the living of cosmic consciousness, or what we are calling here, the attainment of universal being. As I see it, the essence of the journey to universal being has three aspects, and we can call these; intention, initiation and surrender.

It is important to keep in mind that the awakening of cosmic consciousness is a profound spiritual realization that will carry us into a view of reality far beyond anything that we could possibly be prepared for. It is natural for us to imagine this shift in reality to be less than it is. In fact, it is impossible to imagine it otherwise. We can only imagine in terms of reality the way we know it and so any time we attempt to envision a different reality we will inevitably do so in terms of our current reality. There is no way for this not to be the case. A new reality is simply unimaginable. What you will find in this book are some of the ideas that the people who developed the concept of cosmic consciousness used to reshape their own consciousness, and the most important perspectives that have helped me see beyond the familiar into the miraculous. These are not ideas to believe or perspectives to adopt, they are all offered for you to work with, to wrestle with, to play with, so that they can gently begin to open your awareness until the light of cosmic glory begins to shine in.

In whatever form it comes to us, cosmic consciousness is always a shift into a universal identity in which we see that we are not just a small thing in a larger universe. We are the universe itself. We are a cosmic being. You might feel that you understand this, and you very well might. You might even have experienced it before, but there is no way that you can ever be prepared for the direct encounter with it when it arises, or arises again, in front of you. No matter how many times the universal aspect of your nature floods your nervous system with its magnificent expansion of perception, it will always be awesome and overwhelming. In the experience of direct and immediate revelation you may remember previous visitations of the divine, but you will also realize that your memory of those sacred events in no way captures even a small fraction of the reality of them.

The shift to cosmic consciousness is immense, so we must be ready for it. Our so-called spiritual work is whatever we do that prepares us for that impossible leap into novelty, and all of that preparation amounts to one thing, the cultivation of intention. Spiritual work can be defined as whatever effort we must make in the form of practice, study and contemplation, that builds a desire for breakthrough that will propel us beyond reason into the unknown. We must want this transformation with all of our heart. We must be willing to do whatever it takes to invite it into our being and into our lives. We must want to be overwhelmed and ready to receive what we are given.

In a previous book I described what I call the path of spiritual breakthrough as the path that leads to radical transformation through a succession of spiritual openings. The openings do not necessarily occur in order, it is not so much a linear path, as it is a path of expansion. Each new experience opens us in unique ways, expanding our sense of self. As the path of spiritual breakthrough unfolds we receive openings and if we are ready we accept them, open to them, and are transformed by them. The strength of our intention is what invites these openings, and it is also what makes us receptive and ready to be moved by them.

It can be helpful sometimes to anthropomorphize the divine, so throughout this book I will often refer to the divine as a being. I will speak about her perspective on your path. So that you have the chance to see through the eyes of the goal, rather than the eyes of the one seeking - and remember both are you. Relating to the unknowable mystery as a being can open up valuable perspectives on the process of transformation. It also helps us to develop a loving relationship with the miracle that we seek. In terms of intention, imagine that the divine desperately wants to offer you transformative openings. At the same time she knows how precious those openings are and doesn't want to waste them if you don't really want them and are not fully ready to receive them. We can all relate to this. None of us wants to give a valuable gift to someone who doesn't want it, or can't make use of it. You don't give a diamond necklace to a nun, or a sports car to a five year old.

The divine wants us to open, she is passionate about seeing the higher potentials of human consciousness realized. She wants to transform reality and elevate it to new heights and she is always looking for those who are ready to receive her gifts and participate in that process. The divine wants your awakening more than you do. When she sees that you want it as much as she does, she will give you the opportunity. It will not take time. She will respond to your sincere passionate desire for awakening immediately. Again, She wants your awakening more than you do. From this point of view, which is important and powerful although not the only one, the only thing that stands between you and the full reception of the gift of cosmic consciousness is your fully passionate desire for it.

That being said, you can't force yourself to want to awaken more than you actually do. This is not about forcing anything. Awakening cannot be forced. Unfortunately a great deal of the language we have to use is based in a culture that sees everything as an achievement that can be attained through strength of will. Spiritual growth does not happen that way. Spiritual growth happens according to mysterious forces and invisible movements of spirit. You cannot awaken yourself any more than you can control the weather, but that doesn't mean you are not an active participant in the process. Your participation and active engagement is essential, but not in the way you might typically think.

You cannot awaken yourself, but you can open yourself to be

awakened, and being able to discern the difference is essential. Your spiritual work involves opening yourself to the possibility of cosmic consciousness and universal being. It is not something that you do forcefully through effort. In fact, it happens through the relinquishment of effort, but it is something that must be done actively. This unavoidable paradox must be embraced. In order to be open and receptive to the miracle you so passionately desire, you must actively release all of your efforts to attain it while at the same time being willing to make whatever effort is necessary to do this. There are three essential ways that we can cultivate intention in ourselves, through practice, contemplation, and study.

There are many different forms of spiritual practice. Meditation has been the single most important form for me, but I have also been involved with movement based practices like yoga and prostrations, as well as breathing practices, mantra practices, and many others. In the fruition of all spiritual practice is the surrender of all effort. The adept practitioner of any form will be the one who does the practice without effort. They will simply surrender to the meditation, or the mantra, or the pose.

The goal of all of our spiritual work in the form of practice, contemplation, and study, is to intensify our passion for transformation, invite breakthrough experiences into our lives, and build our capacity to surrender to whatever we experience. This is the aspect of spiritual life in which we must make whatever effort is necessary to succeed. Of course, we must always remember that the effort we make is all in service of becoming more and more willing to make no effort at all. The beginning and end of spiritual life is surrender. Surrender means letting go of all effort, however, paradoxically for most of us, it takes a lot of effort to come to a place where we are finally willing to make no effort at all.

As the spiritual path unfolds we experience openings, breakthroughs and revelations. These shifts in perspectives initiate us into new potentials. Each time we find that our consciousness opens to another dimension of reality, we come in contact with new possibilities. What is so exciting about spiritual experiences is not simply how they feel, it is what they reveal to us. These moments of elevated awareness show us that we are more than we thought and that more is possible for us than we ever imagined.

The initiation into cosmic consciousness reveals the potential for human life to be lived from a profound recognition of oneness. In that experience we see that ultimately we are an awakening cosmos that has clothed itself in an individual identity, but is not limited to that identity. We see that we were alive before we were born in human form, and we will live beyond the completion of this human lifetime. We know beyond doubt that we are infinite and eternal. We also recognize that everyone else is that same infinite and eternal self and we are all one. The possibility of a human future in which everyone is living from the direct recognition that we are all one is what broke Edward Carpenter's heart wide open and became the driving vision for all of the work he would engage with throughout his entire life.

Spiritual work, if done with sincerity and dedication, will inevitably lead to spiritual openings. These openings reveal new possibilities for living. Once the door of a new possibility opens, it is up to us to step through that door by allowing our lives to be shaped by it. Edward Carpenter, as we will soon see, was willing to do this. He pursued spiritual openings and when he had them he followed them wherever they led. It is possible to have a spiritual opening and not follow it, but if we don't, the revelation and the potential that it revealed will fade into memory and eventually disappear. When a door opens we must walk through or it will close and we will be left with nothing but a memory.

Of course, by using the metaphor of walking through a door, I am implying that there is something effortful to surrender when there is not. You see, surrender is a natural and necessary result of the spiritual opening itself. Don't think of a door opening in front of you to step through. Think of a trap door opening up in the floor under your feet. Falling through the opening in the floor is not something you do, it is a natural outcome of the opening. If the ground falls away from beneath you, you will fall. You do not have to do anything to fall. It is a natural and necessary consequence of the hole. The only way to avoid falling is to hold on somewhere and stop yourself. So when a spiritual door opens under your feet it is crucial that you let go, fall in, and don't hold on.

Spiritual openings are always overwhelming, and when they come the most natural thing for us to do is to react to them by contracting and holding ourselves back. We see a new universe opening up. We feel ourselves falling into it. We panic and contract, maybe just ever so slightly pulling away. We in effect deny what we have seen, or at least deny the significance of it. We convince ourselves that it is too much for us, or that we can't do it, or that we are unworthy of such a blessing. Somehow or other, almost everyone who experiences a deep spiritual breakthrough will react by holding on rather than letting go. When we hold on, even if only for a second, the opening closes.

Another way to understand spiritual work is to see all the practice, contemplation and study that we do as a way of building a very powerful habit of letting go in the face of the transformative opening. When that spiritual opening occurs and the doors of perception open wide, in spite of the overwhelming nature of the experience, it is possible to have developed a habit of release that is so strong that we will naturally let go in that crucial moment rather than hold on. That is another way to understand what spiritual work is all about. We want letting go to become more natural to us than holding on.

When that moment of initiation occurs and our hearts and minds open to the unimaginable, we will see with new eyes. We will have some sense or vision of a magnificent possibility. As we release into that possibility we will find that some things we used to do, some people we used to spend time with, and some ways we used to think, no longer appeal to us. We don't despise them, they simply don't interest us anymore. At the very same time new activities, people and ways of thinking start to look very attractive. Our old way of being, the one we are so habituated to, starts to fall away, and a new way of being, one that is unknown to us, begins to be revealed. All we need to do is allow the transformation to happen. We don't need to force ourselves to change, we simply allow ourselves to be different. Once that revelation has emerged and taken hold inside you, you are different. I suggest not to think of yourself as someone who has seen a possibility that you must live into. Instead, recognize that the person who had the opening, is already a different person, and just be that person.

Now that we have explored the path of spiritual transformation, we will return to the story of Edward Carpenter and discover how the experience of cosmic consciousness came into his life and how he responded to it. As you get to know his story better, you will see yourself in it. We will explore Carpenter's story, not as a matter of historical record, but as a source of inspiration and instruction, and a blueprint for how cosmic consciousness can be lived.

We will start our story somewhere during the years 1868 or 1869, when Carpenter claims he first read Walt Whitman's legendary book of poetry *Leaves of Grass* in an edition published in England. Carpenter would later claim that the poetry in that book would work a revolution within him for years to come. This small detail opens up for us one of the most mysterious elements of spiritual growth and mystical awakening. Reading the book of poetry, by a previously unknown American author, that was as much despised as adored by critics, ignited an inner revolution in him. How? Why? These are questions that Carpenter himself would think deeply about.

Some writing it seems has the power to touch us far more

deeply than any merely intellectual understanding of the words. What Carpenter received from Whitman's poetry was not information, or even knowledge in any common sense. It wasn't even an appreciation of the aesthetic beauty of the work. No, it was something much deeper than all of these that touched him. In spiritual language the mysterious contact that can occur between a book and a reader is sometimes called *transmission*. It is a mysterious process of energetic osmosis through which the experience of the poet is infused into the experience of the reader. This crucial component of the spiritual path is mysterious for two reasons. First, there is no visible mechanism for the exchange that occurs - it is not the understanding of the words alone that carries the crucial meaning. It is possible to receive a transmission from a text that you only partially understand, and the ambiguity of meaning that is a hallmark of poetic verse ensures that the true meaning of a poem always exists beyond the literal meaning of the words. The second reason for the mystery is that the exchange happens selectively. Not everyone that reads a piece is affected by it. The reason why one person's life is transformed by a poem and another puts it down without being touched at all, can never be completely understood.

Transmission is a part of every spiritual path. It is the mysterious sharing of an understanding that cannot be contained in words. When transmission has occurred the one who receives the transmission knows that they have received something of ultimate value. They know that their life will never be the same, but when they try to explain what they received to someone else they find that there is no way to describe it adequately. It can be exceedingly frustrating to have understood something of such tremendous value and feel completely ill equipped to share it.

Of course this difficulty in sharing our most ephemeral experiences is not always the case. Any of us who feel they have something of depth to share will occasionally find a person who understands exactly what we are describing. They seem almost to already know, or at least to be profoundly predisposed to knowing. This predisposal to the subtle transmissions is another essential aspect of the spiritual path. As we progress spiritually, we are opening to new dimensions of reality. We cannot find our way there by walking a prescribed path. We are moving into the unknown and so the path we follow to find our way there is equally mysterious. Yes, we can engage with practices, contemplate, and study, and these do in a mysterious way make us more open to transmission, but the transmission itself will always come to us from a place we cannot see.

Carpenter was open to the spiritual transmission that Walt Whitman had infused into his poetry. There were others who received this transmission and some of them gathered around Whitmam as disciples around a teacher. Richard Maurice Bucke was one of these and later Carpenter joined that intimate circle. Whitman was a primary inspiration for both men throughout their lives. The question we want to ask now is, why? Why was Carpenter open to receive the transmission? Why was he receptive to the inner revelation that *Leaves of Grass* would ignite within him? This is a question that fascinated Carpenter. He wrote about and contemplated why it was that some books that you read can easily be put down and forgotten, while others grab hold of you until you find yourself reading and rereading them, and they always seem to have more to say and are never any less fresh and alive. Each reading of such a book brings with it a new set of insights equally profound to those that came before. These powerful books become lifelong companions and guides on the path.

I am personally very familiar with this phenomenon because, like Carpenter, I too experienced a life changing inner revelation from reading a book. As a young man I was obsessed with spiritual ideas and perspectives. I practiced vipassana meditation which I learned mainly from books and my association with the Cambridge Insight Meditation Center in Massachusetts. I was reading an enormous number of books on meditation, mysticism, philosophy and psychology. I meditated daily and did weekend retreats at the center in Cambridge. I found many of the books I read fascinating and I had many moments of insight and deepening of understanding over a few years, but nothing that I encountered was life changing until one day in a spiritual bookstore I saw a photograph of a spiritual teacher on a poster announcing that he would be teaching in the area. I looked at the photo and saw a very happy looking man. My experience of Buddhist practice was that it was serious and a little bland. Happiness was not something I associated with my spiritual path. I thought about depth, fulfillment and enlightenment, but not happiness. My imagination was completely captivated by this photo. I kept looking at it and wondering about the radiant joy that seemed to be shining through the photo. I had received a transmission. I did not know it at the time, but that photo would change my life.

Remember that we spoke about the spiritual path unfolding through successive stages of intention, initiation, and surrender. The few years I had spent reading spiritual books, meditating, and visiting my local meditation center had built my intention. I wanted more. I really wanted more. And that passionate desire for more was a huge part of what had made me ready to receive the transmission from that photo. My fascination with the photo was the initiation. I couldn't have realized it at the time, but that photo was a doorway to a life different than any I had ever imagined for myself. The door was open and now it was up to me to step through.

The final stage of the process is surrender, which generally means that a response is required. I could be prepared to receive the transmission, I could actually receive it, and I could still ignore it and do nothing. I could have walked out of that bookstore and forgotten about it. Afterall, it was only an advertising flier and I had ignored hundreds of those before, but not this time. Instead, I went up to the counter and asked the person working there if they knew who that teacher was and if they had any books by them. They did not, but they could order one for me. That was it. That was my response to the poster. Surrender is a big fancy spiritual word, and in some circumstances it means acting in some large and profound way, but at other times it simply means taking the next logical step. After becoming fascinated by that photo, the next logical step was to find out more about the person in it by ordering a copy of the book he had written. Ordering a copy of that book might not look like a life transforming event, but soon I would see that it was. That photo had initiated an inner revolution in my soul that would dramatically shape the rest of my life, right up to the moment of writing this book.

I will never forget the day the book arrived at the store where I had ordered it and I went to pick it up. I had many errands that I needed to do that day. I was picking up things from various stores in preparation for some yard work I had planned to do. I decided to make my first stop at the bookstore. The book was called *Enlightenment is a Secret* and it was written by a spiritual teacher named Andrew Cohen that I knew nothing about.

As I said, reading this book changed my life. It ignited a series of events that led to my living in Cohen's spiritual community for twenty years, acting as his personal assistant for over a decade, and becoming a prominent teacher in my own right. My association with him was profoundly impactful, but I cannot mention his name without reservation. He was a complicated man, filled with incongruent aspects of his personality. In the end his personal failings led to the collapse of the community that had grown up around him. The long and complicated story of the genius and madness that I experienced during those twenty years is much too involved to go into here, but I feel I must qualify what I will share in recognition of the complexity of the story as a whole and perhaps as a word of caution regarding the challenging world of spiritual authority.

With that disclaimer, I can say that something profound happened to me when I read *Enlightenment is a Secret*, which I finished the same day that I bought it. I remember vividly how I walked out of the store with my new book in my hand, sat down on a stone sidewalk that surrounded the store and read the first few pages. As soon as I started reading I felt the power in its words. The book was made up of short passages, most of them less than a page long. I didn't even understand a great deal of what they said. Of course I knew the meaning of the words in the English language, but the sentences, metaphors and descriptions of inner revelation were often beyond my ability to grasp. What was unmistakable to me was that each passage no matter what it said brought my attention back to the center of my own soul. I had never been affected by a book like that. It didn't matter that I didn't understand everything that was being explained. The energy behind the words was moving me, affecting my perception, and returning me again and again to a place inside me that had no beginning and no end, that existed beyond the bounds of time and space, and was the true source of my being.

I read outside the store until the excitement in my body was so great that I had to stop and give myself a break. Then I would drive to the next stop on my list, do whatever I needed to do there, and find a quiet place to read again until the energy in my body was more than I could stand. Throughout the day I read the whole book this way and by the end of that day I was utterly resigned to the fact that I would meet the author.

I had another, more recent, experience of spiritual transmission through the written word after meeting a woman named Jody Mountain in Hawaii. She was a lineage holder in the spiritual body work tradition of Ancient Lomi Lomi and when I received a massage from her I knew that I had experienced something beyond any physical contact I had known before. I had received a transmission of the lineage of Lomi Lomi through the massage. During the sixty minutes of bodywork that I had received, I felt that my body and her hands were communicating as she touched me. Our minds were not involved in the communication, one body was communicating directly with another. It was extraordinary.

Once I was home again I spent a lovely day at a friend's house reading some blog posts I found on Jody's website. As soon as I started reading I felt a powerful energy building in my body. I found that I could only read one post before the energy would build to an intensity that was uncomfortable and I would jump in the pool. After a few minutes in the cool water I would read another blog post. I spent the afternoon reading through a dozen of her posts. By the time I was done I had resolved to do one of Jody's ten-day training sessions. I ended up training twice with her, one in Hawaii and one in Ireland. I learned to give Lomi Lomi massages and over the next two years gave nearly two hundred massages. The original initiation had come in the transmission I received during a massage rather than from a photograph and again my response was to find out more about the person involved by reading what they had written. And once again that simple act of surrender had profound effects on me.

I have not seen anywhere that Edward Carpenter describes his first reading of Walt Whitman in detail, but I imagine that he might have had an experience something like mine. He was certainly captivated by the poems that he read and claimed they had initiated an inner revolution within him. Less than a decade after reading the book, Carpenter made the long sea voyage to the United States to visit the man whose writing had ignited a fire in his mind, body and soul. Meeting Whitman brought his initiation to a new level of depth because he found in the poet a man who matched his writings. Carpenter realized that it was Whitman's being that was transmitted through those poems as much as anything else. He felt that he had found in Whitman a superior possibility for being human and he felt that supporting the cultivation of individuals who exhibited exemplary human character was the ultimate purpose of life and should be the ultimate goal of governments. His recognition of higher human potentials, along with his realization that those possibilities are equally available to all of us, became the foundation of a life devoted, in large part, to social activism.

Over the next few years Carpenter would be moved by what he had experienced. He contemplated higher human possibilities and wrote down short phrases and passages as they came to his mind. There was no coherent throughline connecting what he was writing, but as they were arising spontaneously from his inner revolution, he faithfully recorded the various passages that came to him. A few years after meeting Whitman, Carpenter received a copy of the *Bhagavad Gita*, a sacred Hindu text. What he discovered in this holy book was the keynote that allowed everything he had been contemplating to fall into place. He found himself drenched in a mood of exaltation and inspiration that he described as a kind of super-consciousness. This keynote consciousness harmonized all of his thoughts and feelings and resulted in the birth of his own book of inspired poetry called *Towards Democracy*.

Carpenter built a small "sentinel box" outside of his home to write in. I imagine him in a space even smaller than Henry Thoreau's cabin, but serving much the same purpose. In that small shelter, Carpenter would write, often until late at night, by candlelight. He wrote spontaneously as inspiration moved him. Today we might describe the poems as a download from spirit. Carpenter's small book of poems didn't find a wide audience, though it was certainly revered by some. The great twentieth century Hindu sage Sri Aurobindo was adamant about the value of Carpenter's poetry and placed him along with Whitman as examples of a new trend in poetry. Aurobindo also claimed that Carpenter's poetry was an even higher expression of the Self than Whitman's had been.

The cycle of initiation and surrender was not yet complete for Carpenter and the notion of cosmic consciousness was not born in the pages of *Towards Democracy*. That final fruition would need to wait another decade before Carpenter would receive an invitation from a friend he had met in college to come to Ceylon (modern day Sri Lanka) where he would meet a holy man of India. Carpenter responded to that invitation by making another long trip, this time from England to Ceylon where he would spend six weeks in the daily company of a guru named Ramaswamy.

For the second time in his life, Carpenter found himself in the presence of a remarkable human being who seemed to represent a higher possibility that all of us could achieve. Ramaswamy appears to have been on a solitary retreat living in a small chamber that he generally left for only one half hour a day. Carpenter described this deeply spiritual man as having the qualities of profound sense of open softness, coupled with a penetrating mental clarity. The swami could speak endlessly on matters of spirit when asked to, but when there were no questions to answer and no need to attend to anything external, his attention would immediately turn inward. He would pass many hours in quiet inner contemplation and his eyes would reveal the distant gaze that overcomes one when they are focused on matters of spirit.

In the presence of the powerful swami, a spiritual cycle came to completion. Carpenter would go on to describe the esoteric mystical philosophy of India as a tradition which is aimed at the attainment of a new order of consciousness that he called cosmic consciousness. This was not a phrase he had heard, nor was it a literal translation of what he had been taught. It was simply the best phrase he could come up with in his native language of English to describe what he discovered in Ceylon. He believed he had come up with a phrase that reasonably captured what he had understood about the Hindu conceptions of sat-chit-ananda (existence-consciousness-bliss) and the unified consciousness of

Brahman. Carpenter was trying to present the wisdom of the East as much as he was trying to share what he experienced as the completion of a spiritual cycle that had begun nearly a decade and a half earlier when he read *Leaves of Grass*.

Now he knew what he had felt calling to him through the poems of Whitman's book, and what he had seen in the character of Whitman, and now in Ramaswamy. It was cosmic consciousness. There were practices and teachings that lead to this heightened perception, but there could be no definitively prescribed path because everyone's needs on the path are unique and the wisdom of the esoteric tradition must be applied appropriately to the exact needs of the individual. There was no fast track to cosmic consciousness, no quick route to enlightenment. Carpenter saw this as an evolutionary leap both personally and culturally. Cosmic consciousness represented a new level of consciousness emerging from a cosmic identity. There are those who have arrived in this new mind sooner than the rest, but it is everyone's destiny. Carpenter believed he was seeing the future of consciousness in Whitman and Ramaswamy. This new consciousness will take many generations to become fully established on Earth, and it will bring with it a new and unimaginable world that will need to be lived and explored for years beyond that.

Carpenter outlined his evolutionary view of cosmic consciousness in *From Adam's Peak to Elephanta*. He would describe human evolution in terms of a progression from simple-consciousness, to self-consciousness, to cosmic-consciousness. The psychologist Richard Maurice Bucke would expand upon this progression later in his own book on cosmic consciousness As we shall soon see, Bucke's book would offer a much more psychological approach to the topic with very little reference to the Eastern tradition.

Right now I want to return to the main point of this chapter, outlining the path to cosmic consciousness. We described the path as consisting of three elements: intention, initiation, and surrender. We went on to describe initiation in terms of the mysterious ways that higher possibilities call to us from behind the words of a poem, or any form of art, and also through spiritual teachings and those who have become representative examples of those teachings. Now I want you to relate your own experience to this description of the path.

First of all I want to be clear that if you are reading this book then you have already been initiated. You have already heard the call of a higher possibility. And since you have already heard that call, it is likely that in some way or another, consciously or unconsciously, you have built the sensitivity to hear that call as well as some capacity to surrender to it. The fact that you found this book attractive enough to read it proves that to be the case. Deciding to purchase and read this book was an act of surrender to the call. This book occurred to you as potentially valuable enough to devote some of your time and energy to it because you thought that it might take you one step closer to something you have already been pursuing. Cosmic consciousness has been calling you and you the potential of this book to help you find it.

The point here is that cosmic consciousness is already in contact with you. It is already calling and you have already recognized it to some extent. I want you now to look for it in your personal spiritual history. Think about what you were seeking already that made this book attractive to read. This book is the most recent step on your path. What is it a path to? When did you first feel the possibility of cosmic consciousness? It might have been in a different book, or a poem, or a person. It might have been a circumstance, an illness, an accident, the loss of a loved one. Of course it might also have been a spiritual experience, an opening of your heart and mind that temporarily revealed something that you could not forget. It might not be so specific. It might be a certain time in your life when you started wondering about life's meaning and began to ask questions that started you down a road of existential inquiry. It could come in many forms, but you can be sure that it came to you. You are here now reading this book because you have been called. You have been initiated.

Do your best to identify when and how you were called. Recognize that as your initiation. You were almost certainly already looking for something before then, probably without realizing that you were doing spiritual work, but after your initiation you most likely began to consciously look for more. Can you see what it is that called you? If you begin to see that you have been called, you will also see that you are still being called. Cosmic consciousness is still calling to you, still guiding you. If you look, you will find it. It may be an energetic movement in your body, or a deep sense of extraordinary possibility. It might even be a memory of a vision of higher awareness. Whatever it is, find it. Find it and meditate on it. Allow yourself to see it more clearly. As you do, it will grow inside you. You will see that you have been on this path for a long time, and you will rejoice that you have remembered why you are here.

SUMMARY OF EXERCISES

Think again about what attracted you to read this book. Do your best to identify when and how you were called to read it and recognize that as your initiation. Can you see that cosmic consciousness that called you to read this book? Allow whatever it was that called you to read this book to grow inside you. What happens as it grows?

Describe in a notebook or journal about what you see in this investigation.

CHAPTER FIVE

The Evolution of Consciousness

"The real voyage of discovery consists not in seeking new landscapes but in having new eyes."

- Marcel Proust

EDWARD CARPENTER EMBARKED ON A long journey of discovery that eventually led to the invention of the phrase cosmic consciousness. Carpenter had first shared his vision of cosmic consciousness in *Towards Democracy*, but that book did not find a wide audience. It was over a decade later that he wrote about his travels through India and Ceylon and first used the phrase cosmic consciousness. The book of his travel adventures did not attain mass appeal, but it did have some important readers and the most important was Carpenter's friend and fellow disciple, Walt Whitman and Richard Maurice Bucke.

In 1901 Bucke published his now classic work *Cosmic Consciousness: A Study in the Evolution of the Human Mind*. In that book, Bucke expressed his understanding and experience of this exalted state of consciousness and we see a great deal of Carpenter's ideas in Bucke's book, but with a significant difference in emphasis. Bucke was a psychologist and a scientist and his treatment of the subject is similarly psychological and scientific. This is not to say that he was not writing from his own experience. He certainly was. In fact, Bucke's description of his own awakening to cosmic consciousness is one of the most powerful descriptions I have ever seen. I will share with you here that experience as described by Bucke himself and quoted in William James' *The Varieties of Religious Experience*.

> *I had spent the evening in a great city, with two friends, reading and discussing poetry and philosophy. We parted*

at midnight. I had a long drive in a hansom to my lodging. My mind, deeply under the influence of the ideas, images, and emotions called up by the reading and talk, was calm and peaceful. I was in a state of quiet, almost passive enjoyment, not actually thinking, but letting ideas, images, and emotions flow of themselves, as it were, through my mind. All at once, without warning of any kind, I found myself wrapped in a flame-colored cloud. For an instant I thought of fire, an immense conflagration somewhere close by in that great city; the next, I knew that the fire was within myself. Directly afterward there came upon me a sense of exultation, of immense joyousness accompanied or immediately followed by an intellectual illumination impossible to describe. Among other things, I did not merely come to believe, but I saw that the universe is not composed of dead matter, but is, on the contrary, a living Presence; I became conscious in myself of eternal life. It was not a conviction that I would have eternal life, but a consciousness that I possessed eternal life then; I saw that all men are immortal; that the cosmic order is such that without any peradventure all things work together for the good of each and all; that the foundation principle of the world, of all the worlds, is what we call love, and that the happiness of each and all is in the long run absolutely certain. The vision lasted a few seconds and was gone; but the memory of it and the sense of the reality of what it taught has remained during the quarter of a century which has since elapsed. I knew that what the vision showed was true. I had attained a point of view from which I saw that it must be true. That view, that conviction, I may say that consciousness has never, even during periods of the deepest depression, been lost.

Bucke is certainly describing a profound experience and one

that guided the work of his entire life. He was also a devotee of Walt Whitman and like Carpenter, credits the great poet with giving him his initial transmission of comic consciousness in the pages of *Leaves of Grass*. But unlike Carpenter, he did not have a strong connection with the teachings of the East.

In his book Bucke outlines a view of the evolution of consciousness that continued to develop through the twentieth century as a spiritual movement that is often referred to as evolutionary spirituality. Bucke's ideas were echoed and amplified by William James, and both he and Edward Carpenter influenced the Russian mystic P. D. Ouspensky, and the Indian sage Sri Aurobindo. A similar vision of the evolution of consciousness would also be developed by Peirre Teilhard de Chardin whose idea of the noosphere might roughly be equated to cosmic consciousness. And in more recent times luminaries such as Thomas Berry, Barbara Marx Hubbard and Ken Wilber have further expanded on the idea.

Bucke offers a simple model for the evolution of consciousness that offers a very tangible way to grasp the idea. There are three forms of consciousness in existence on this planet, simple-consciousness, self-consciousness, and cosmic-consciousness. A similar set of distinctions was also proposed by Edward Carpenter, but Bucke goes into much greater psychological detail in describing exactly how each form of consciousness evolved into being. I will explain each briefly and refer the curious reader back to Bucke's original book for more details.

Simple-consciousness is the consciousness of sensation and reaction. This consciousness is capable of responding to external stimuli, but only in an unconscious way. A plant may turn towards the light of the sun, but presumably it does not know, at least in the human sense, what it is doing. Simple forms of life exhibit this consciousness and in the most basic way demonstrate an awareness of the world.

It is important to remember that it is very difficult from our anthropocentric point of view to attribute levels of consciousness to other species. We cannot help but see consciousness in relation to our own experience of it. We see other species as conscious to the extent that they exhibit consciousness that matches our own. It is always possible that another species has a completely different type of consciousness, or a consciousness similar to ours but expressed in a vastly different way. In either case we would be unable to recognize it. This is a limitation of our consciousness that is very difficult to entirely avoid. Bucke falls prey to it often, making statements in his book about other species, or even races of humans, that grate tremendously on the modern ear. In my annotated edition of his classic book, I attempted to make some corrections for this, and in this book I will do my best to avoid falling into the same trap.

With that disclaimer let us boldly continue with our exploration. The next form of consciousness is self-consciousness. This consciousness includes the ability to respond to stimuli, but with the addition of understanding what is happening. Self-consciousness is the kind of consciousness that you and I have. We are not just aware of a glass of water, we are also aware that it is a glass of water. In addition, we are aware that we are aware of it. The blind reactive capacity of simple consciousness, through virtue of a sense of self, now becomes a threefold consciousness in which there is awareness of an object, awareness about the object, and awareness of ourselves. William James would explore this threefold nature of consciousness in great depth in his philosophical and psychological works.

Cosmic consciousness is a form of consciousness that Bucke sees exhibited in certain rare individuals throughout history, including a few that were alive in his own time. He includes both Walt Whitman and Edward Carpenter in his very short list of fully realized individuals. Cosmic consciousness, which is the subject of this book, emerges from a deep recognition of the oneness of the cosmos. Bucke's experience of cosmic consciousness, quoted above, provides a wonderful description of exactly what this experience reveals.

Now that I have explained the essentials of these different realms of consciousness I want to guide you into an inner exploration of them. Remember, my intention is to create a practical guide, not an academic study. Those of us who aspire to experience and ultimately live from cosmic consciousness will need to do more than understand how consciousness evolves. We need to feel it. Feeling, not understanding, is the key ingredient to spiritual transformation. In fact, we might use the term "knowing" in a higher sense to mean the combination of a deep understanding of, and a deep feeling for, the truth.

Imagine what the experience of simple-consciousness is like from the inside out. Imagine that you are a creature that can only respond to the light of the sun by turning toward it. You have no thought process, you don't know what you are doing. You don't even know that you exist. The sensation of the light of the sun triggers an instinctive movement towards it. It isn't quite the same as how the wind moves the leaves in a tree, because the leaves are not actively participating in that process, they are being forced to move, at the same time the reactions of simple-consciousness are just a short step removed from those rustling leaves. The difference being that the responses of simple-consciousness occur as the result of an outside stimulus that triggers an internal reaction, in the case of the current example, to the light of the sun. The creature with simple-consciousness is doing something, but what it is doing is reflexive, like your leg jerking when the doctor taps on your knee.

As a creature blessed with simple-consciousness you react to the light of the sun, and that reaction proves that there is sensitivity to the sensation of light, but there is no understanding of it. There are no thoughts about a sun up in the sky, or about light. There are also no thoughts about yourself, your desire for light, the value of light, or anything else. There is a sensation and an automatic reaction to that sensation. That is simple-consciousness. Imagine being that kind of creature. Of course, it is impossible to imagine it because to imagine it you would have to have some idea of what it would be like, and a creature like that has no idea. Still, do your best however you can to feel into that level of consciousness.

Now we want to move on to feeling into our own self-consciousness, which is much easier because it is the kind of consciousness we are intimately familiar with. Imagine your own experience of consciousness. Notice right now how you are aware of the book you are holding in your hands, you are aware that it is a book, and you are aware of yourself as you hold it. Those are the three fundamental components of self-consciousness, awareness of the object, understanding of the object, awareness of yourself.

Bucke points out that self-consciousness necessitates language. You cannot have self-conscious awareness prior to the advent of language. I want to caution that I do not feel that this has to imply human language - other species may have other forms of language, which means other ways of representing the world in symbolic form. If we extend Bucke's point beyond human language we would simply say that for self-consciousness to arise some form of language is required and it will be useful for us to go into some detail as to why that is the case.

Self-consciousness and language are inseparably one. They are flip sides of a single coin. This is because it is language that gives us the ability to hold abstract meaning. This is an important point to move slowly through. Language gives us the opportunity to understand things in a symbolic form. As we have already seen, the word cat means something in the sense that it stands for a furry little animal. If there are three different things in front of me and I ask you to point to the cat, you will not point to the basketball or the notebook, you will point to the cat. Having done so, we can safely conclude that you *understand* what a cat is. It is important to remember that when we say that we understand what a cat is, what we really mean is that I understand what the word *cat* represents in the world. This form of understanding makes language possible.

The miracle of language is that it allows us to represent things that exist in the world in the mental form of words, and that understanding can be held in our own mind and shared with the minds of others. Any of us who have played charades knows how difficult it is to convey ideas without the use of language, and if you count gesturing and miming as forms of language, which they are, then it would be impossible to convey anything without them. Language is what allows us to represent things in the world in the form of symbols. Language not only allows us to communicate ideas, language allows us to know things in the form of understanding them - which means knowing the reality that stands underneath the words we use.

Imagine that you have no language at all. Look around you and imagine that you had no language, no words to represent anything. You simply have the pure sensual experience of seeing what is in front of you and no way of knowing what any of it is. You would not be able to recognize anything in the sense of being able to name it. Notice that the word *recognize* comes from re-cognize, or to know again. You know something once when you have a purely sensational experience of it, you know it again when you have some form of language that allows you to understand what it is in a symbolic form.

We only have to think for a moment to see how dramatically our experience changes once language is introduced into our consciousness. One helpful way to think about this is to contemplate how we live in a conceptual world. Look around you, what do you see? You see things, identifiable things, things like chairs, tables and trees. But you have to remember a chair is only a chair if you know what it is. If you took a chair and dropped it into a culture where they had no idea what a chair was, it would just be a thing. If you saw an artifact from another culture and you didn't know what it was, it would just be a thing. To someone from that culture it would be obvious that it was more than just a thing, it was a very particular thing. You might try to guess at what it was. You might try to sit on it to see if it was a chair of some kind. But you would only be guessing.

Everything around you that you can recognize is a conceptualized thing. That is why I say that we live in a conceptual world. A world that is infused with language. A world where everything is something that is symbolically conveyed in the word that names it. As we go deeper into our exploration of a radically different experience of consciousness we need to look closely at our current experience. Ask yourself, how much of your daily experience is conceptualized. We experience sensations. We experience the color, the hardness, and the shape of the chair, but we also experience the chair, you could almost say the chairness of it. If you think about it, you will begin to see that a great deal of your experience is really the experience of concepts and ideas.

If we are talking about obvious things like chairs or trees, this all seems a bit trivial, but simple things are only a small part of our experience. When we think of more complex things, like cars, or schools, we begin to see lots of separate things all lumped together. If we think about a forest, a monetary system, or an ecosystem, things get even more complex. It seems relatively easy to find the border that creates a car. We know what is, and what is not, a car, but an ecosystem is much more complex. It doesn't have easily identifiable edges that define it. The more complex a thing is, the more abstract it becomes. How about money? Is this piece of paper in my hand with the printing on it really valuable? It is as long as I am exchanging it with someone who recognizes the value of it. The point here is just to think about all this. See the world around you as deeply conceptualized. All of the things you can see can be represented in words. Having the right words to describe things in the world is what we mean by understanding something. When I ask you a question, you demonstrate that you understand what I am saying by using the right words in response. I want to know if you understand me. That means I want to know if your mind is envisioning the same thing that my mind is when we say the same words. I give you words that describe what is in my mind, and you speak words that give me confidence that you have the same thing in your mind.

The development of language opens up a new world for us because it makes abstract thinking possible. This advancement in consciousness was beautifully described by David Abrams in his book, *The Spell of the Sensuous*. I want to take you through a little of what he explained in that book because it will help us gain a better understanding of the reality we live in and how it is created. One of the things that Bucke placed great emphasis on in his book was the huge gulf that separated simple consciousness from self-consciousness, and then again from self-consciousness to cosmic consciousness. This I believe is also important for our exploration because it will help us understand how the journey to the cosmic is attained.

Let's take our exploration of language and consciousness a little further before turning our attention to the sense of self that forms out of language. In *The Spell of the Sensuous*, Abrams explains that language in its simplest forms, is directly representational. We can use the example of pointing your finger. Imagine that you point your finger at the moon as in the famous Eastern teaching analogy. This could be seen as a very simple language in which you are bringing someone's attention to the moon by pointing towards it. This may seem like an obvious gesture to us, but if you think about it, the person seeing you point your finger needs to know that pointing a finger is a sign meant to direct your attention at the object being pointed to. If the person doesn't know to follow the direction in which the finger is pointing, they will simply be staring at a hand with one finger out, and missing the moon.

According to Abrams, early forms of languages were made up of very direct symbols. Three wavy lines drawn on a page might represent water. A circle might represent the sun. With a language this immediate everything needs to have its own symbol to represent it. The language quickly becomes huge and cumbersome. As language developed something amazing happened, alphabets. This new kind of language used a very different kind of written symbol. Instead of having a different written symbol for each thing represented, each set of letters represented a different basic sound element. Now you could create combined symbols, i.e., words for everything, by simply combining a small number of written symbols.

What is important to see here is that the economy of form offered by alphabetic languages meant that many more things could be symbolically represented. Language that utilizes an alphabet is one step removed from reality. The symbols of the language do not directly represent things, they represent sounds and then combinations of sounds formed words that represent things. The earlier language was created from symbols that pointed directly at things in the world, alphabets use letters that point to sounds made in our mouths and those sounds point to things in the world.

Abrams points out that languages utilizing alphabets had the unanticipated negative impact of separating us from direct contact with the world around us. He feels that this is one of the factors that has led our species to be able to create so much damage to our natural environment without realizing that we are hurting ourselves in the process.

At the same time, the level of abstraction in language opened doors to a seemingly unlimited number of things that could be symbolically represented. Not only could we create symbols for things like water, cats, moons, and grandmothers, but we could also represent things like social justice, racial equity, and spiritual awakening. And we could use many words to describe things in minute detail, in the way that I am using all the words in this book to bring you into contact with the reality of cosmic consciousness.

The world that opened up for us when we moved from consciousness without language to consciousness with language is immense. The leap between the world of a creature that only possesses the reactive capacity to respond to stimuli, to the world of a creature who can use a complex language to create abstract symbols for an infinite number of things, both physical and mental, is unfathomable.

Again take a moment to contemplate how much of your reality is conceptual. How much of what you experience is made possible because you have language and words. Look around and imagine that you didn't have any language. You would see all the things in the room around you, but you wouldn't know what any of it was. I am sitting in a room and if I had no language I would have no way of knowing that I was typing on a computer. I would certainly have no idea what these words mean that sit on my screen. I wouldn't know what country I was in, or how to create a book out of these words that could be distributed all over the world. I wouldn't know that I lived in a world in the first place. It is hard to imagine that any of the technology we use, aside from perhaps simple hand tools, would have been developed without the benefit of language. And we haven't even begun to think about all of the sacred texts, stories, myths, fables, novels, poems, and other literature that would not have been written, and could not even have been thought about. You can go on and on. If you could erase the development of language from human history, it is hard to imagine what the world around us would look like.

After reading Abrams first book I was left with a bit of an unsettled feeling. He is very effective in pointing out that our sense of separation from the world we live in, caused in part by the abstract nature of our thinking, can be seen as the root cause of environmental degradation and the climate crisis. Our species followed the abstract power of language to soar up and into heights of thought far from Earth, but in doing so we lost direct contact with the planet that supports us. In his next book, *Becoming Animal*, Abrams shares a revelation. He seems to have realized that we flew off into realms of abstraction to develop all of the magnificent powers and capacities that can be found there, not to destroy our world, but to bring those gifts back to the world. It was necessary that we would fly off into abstraction and develop all of the powers that we could there, but now it is time for us to return to Earth and to bring the powers back to her. These powers were never meant for us, we simply needed to develop them, they were meant for the world and now we must return them. I am personally very moved by the vision that Abrams presents in his second book, and it is my firm conviction that the attainment of cosmic consciousness is how we can return those powers of abstraction back to Earth, and ultimately to the cosmos.

There is just one more step on this journey into language and the power of abstract thinking that I want us to take and it is the most important one. This next step in the story of language brings us directly to the heart of the matter because of all the things that we can think abstractly about, the most significant one is ourselves.

I want to share something before I continue, it is a story about the early Christain saint Augustine. In his autobiography, Augustine shares about his first encounter with silent reading. He and his mother were astonished to see Bishop Ambrose reading without moving his lips. His eyes would scan across the page and he would enter into an inner contemplation of the words. This was shocking because at the time reading was always done out loud. I imagine that it might have generally appeared to people that the words on the page were moving their lips and then they would understand the words as you heard them. This was different, the bishop's lips never moved, no sound was ever heard, and yet the bishop understood anyway.

I present this story to continue to create a sense of the miracle of abstract thinking. What was so miraculous about the bishop's reading was that it happened entirely within the invisible realm of the mind. Before the discovery of silent reading, written words were part of the outside world that could be seen, like trees, cats, and the moon, but now the words were having an effect from within. We can imagine that it is only a short leap from the discovery of silent reading to the development of inner contemplation and thinking. Humanity was beginning, through the magical power of language, to create a vast inner world of understanding that did not just mirror, but enriched the outer world of the physical senses. We could sit alone in our bedroom and contemplate the world because the world could be recognized, or re-cognized, inside us.

The most amazing thing that we could recognize inside is our self. With the growth of our powers of abstraction came the development of an inner conception of ourselves, a self-concept. We could imagine ourselves inside the way we could imagine any other part of reality. The world that we live in is populated with things of all kinds, and we ourselves became one of those things that exists in the world. This ability to see ourselves inside our minds gave us the power to be conscious of ourselves. So much became possible for us with the birth of self-consciousness. We could now imagine ourselves in the world. We could predict how we would be affected by other things and other people. We could project ourselves into the future and decide upon the most powerful course of action. The birth of self-consciousness was a miracle that radically changed what was possible.

The advent of more formalized language was one of the primary drivers of an immense acceleration of human invention. We can debate whether this has had a net positive impact or not, but we cannot deny that it has happened. Our early ancestors had nothing but hand tools at their disposal for over a million years, but look at the world today. Then in just a few thousand years there has been a veritable explosion of invention. A great deal of good has come out of this creative burst, and a great deal of harm has been done too. To me the jury is still out as to what this will all mean in the end. The worst case scenario is the annihilation of all life on our planet, rendering the entire human experiment a useless exercise in self aggrandizement. The best case scenario, the one that I personally am holding out for, is that it all leads to a leap in consciousness in which the creative power of abstract thinking stops being used exclusively for the benefit of just one species and starts being utilized on behalf of the planet and ultimately the cosmos. I believe that cosmic consciousness is one particularly powerful way to understand that leap into a new way of being that will usher in a new acceleration of invention in directions that we are as incapable of imagining as our hand tool wielding ancestors were incapable of understanding our world today. The world that is created from cosmic consciousness is unimaginable and both Richard Maurice Bucke and Edward Carpenter were deeply inspired by the magnificent potential of it.

The birth of an inner sense of self was the keynote of the leap from simple-consciousness to self-consciousness. The advent of the self-concept dramatically expanded what was possible. Let's look carefully into our own experience of self-awareness so that we can understand the miracle that we are in possession of, although we tend to completely take it for granted.

We are trained to understand ourselves as something that can be described in words. I am Jeff. I am a man. I am a writer. All of these sentences, I presume, describe the thing that I am. This skill of self-identification, the ability to identify myself and represent who I am to myself and others, is the distinguishing characteristic of self-consciousness. The development of this capacity must be preceded by the development of language, and by language I simply mean the capacity to use symbols to represent things in the world.

We have established the fact that we live in a conceptual world and as William James said, the most important concept I have is the one I hold about myself. How I see myself is a determining factor of what is possible for me. I saw this very powerfully during the years that I was a special needs teacher. I worked with middle school age children who had various types of mild to moderate learning challenges. What I quickly saw was how much of their supposed inability to learn came not from the very real challenges they face, but from the identity they had developed as someone who could not learn. They could learn, they just needed to learn differently than others, but because they had learned to see themselves as someone who could not learn they didn't even try. They ended up in a negative downward spiral. They believed they could not learn and so they didn't try, because they didn't try they didn't learn, and their identity as someone who could not learn was affirmed and strengthened. I quickly realized that my success as a teacher hinged on my ability to convince my students to at least question their current identity.

In many ways that very same mechanism is at work in my work as a spiritual guide and mentor. The first thing that I need to encourage people to do is question the solidity of their current identity. The leap to cosmic consciousness is the leap beyond our current sense of self. We cannot hold on to who we think we are and move into that miraculous expanded sense of being. This leap beyond our current sense of self is in some traditions referred to as ego death. That is a term that I find harsh, harmful and misleading. Your ego does not have to die in order to leap into a radically different consciousness, in fact I believe, and some would argue the point with me, that as an organizing principle your ego needs to remain intact and healthy. But it needs to become unconscious. We don't need to kill our ego as much as we need to forget about it. I like to refer to this necessity of the spiritual path as self-forgetting.

Think of riding a bike. When you first start riding you have to pay a lot of attention to the process of riding. You have to think about balance, peddling, and steering. You are very consciously riding a bike, but to become proficient you need to move beyond this self-conscious effort. Riding a bike needs to become unconscious and automatic. Then we can ride faster, we can pay attention to the world around us, we can enjoy riding rather than working at it. This is true of any activity that we master. Think of swinging a baseball bat, driving a car, or reading a book. You can't really enjoy a story until you have mastered reading to the point that it happens more or less automatically. If you have to look up the meaning of every other word the process of reading is not much fun.

I see this same principle at play as we make the leap from self-consciousness to cosmic consciousness. An inevitable part of the process is letting go of the sense of self. I do not mean destroying it, I mean forgetting about it and allowing it to operate in the background. We become unaware of our ego, our sense of self, and become available for a radically different reality to emerge in front of us. In this book we are in the process of preparing for that leap by developing a deep understanding of our self-concept, how it is formed and how it operates. This understanding will serve us in moving beyond it..

I think of Jeff as who I am, but Jeff is a concept, an idea about who I am. We all have a self-concept, and that self-concept is very helpful because it allows us to picture ourselves in the world. It is the basis for anticipating the future, decision making, and learning from our experience. It is a very useful tool, but it is not who we are. The recognition that we are not our self-concept, is the fulcrum around which spiritual enlightenment pivots. We are not a self-concept, we are that which perceives the self concept. This recognition is the door that opens us to the possibility of cosmic consciousness. The path to profound spiritual transformation necessitates relaxing our habitual and often obsessive engagement with our self-concept and forgetting about ourselves.

Ask yourself, who are you? Who is the person that responds to your name? You will find that there are many answers. You are a man or a woman. You are a doctor or a grocery store clerk. You are industrious or you are lazy. You are wise or you are foolish. The list of sentences about yourself is infinite, but none of that is who you are. Those are aspects of you, qualities of you, parts of you, but who is the one that all of those parts are pointing to. Anything you can see, imagine or point to, can never be who you are, because you will always be whoever it is that is seeing, imagining or pointing.

Through this magical process of conceptualization we created a concept of ourselves, but then we mistakenly became identified with it. We think we are a concept. We have come to see ourselves as a finger pointing to the moon and forgotten about the moon. William James talked about the distinction between our self-concept and our true self as the difference between "I" and "me". *I* am the one that sees the *me*. The me is myself, or my-self. The me is a self concept that I am aware of. To illustrate this even further, the great philosopher John Dewey talked about how babies are not born knowing who they are, they have to learn who they are. In fact they are not born being anyone. They are just born.

When a baby is born the adults around it choose a name for it and start using that name to refer to it. The baby is now not just a baby, it is a particular baby, a self with a name. The adults repeat the name in the company of the baby over and over again. Then once, by chance, the baby responds to the name by looking, or blinking or smiling. The adults get very excited. It has recognized its name. Of course, in reality the baby hasn't really recognized anything, it has simply responded to a sound it has heard repeatedly. The adults are thrilled. They reward the baby with excited attention and so the baby learns to respond to that sound. The adults will speak as if the baby knows her name, but that isn't really true yet.

Eventually the baby develops a very strong habit of responding to the name it has been given. Now whenever Dawn hears her name, she responds in some way. Responding to our name becomes a lifelong habit. We still all do it. If I hear my name I turn. I listen. I respond. I do that thinking it is because I know that name refers to me, which is true, but Dewey wants us to also see that what we think of as knowing who I am, started - and is still largely - a habit of responding to the sound of your name.

Our habit of self-conceptualization started when we were conditioned to respond to our name. Once we learned to use language we then learned many things about the person that name referred to. One of the great powers of psychology is the recognition that many of things that we learned about ourselves impede our ability to live healthy full lives. Part of the psychological process of therapy involves uncovering the unhealthy aspects of our self-concept, recognizing that they are not who we are, and then developing healthy and supportive replacements.

The important thing to consider here is the fact that there was no self there at the start. There was just a baby. Babies are not born with a self-concept, they learn one. They learn that they are a specific person with certain attributes. They are capable of some things and not others, but to a large extent, our self-concept is just a habitual way of seeing ourselves and our psychological growth often involves breaking certain habitual ways of seeing ourselves and replacing them with better ways.

Esoteric spiritual practices hinge on a wholesale release of the sense of self. The foundational belief that a self-concept rests on, is the belief that it refers to who we are. We believe that our self-concept points to us. We essentially believe that we are that. Spiritual enlightenment always includes, and is initiated by, the realization that you are not who you think you are. You are not a thing that can be labeled with a concept. You are a mystery that cannot be limited to any concept. You are the source. This realization of our True Self is a shift into a completely different reality. In this book you will see that it is the initiating point that can lead to the realization of cosmic consciousness.

There is one more perspective on the sense of self that is valuable for us to consider, this time from William James. James termed the sense of self arising within the *stream of consciousness*. James realized that from our perception as human beings the only thing that exists is the unending flow of our experience. This is what he called the stream of consciousness. Our experience of reality is an unending experience of awareness. We are aware of one thing after another. I have found this to be a very valuable insight to work with. Pay attention to your experience right now and you will see that it is composed entirely of experiences that occur in a continuous unfolding. The continuous flow of experience includes being aware of things outside yourself in the world, the thoughts and feelings that exist in your mind, and finally the sense of being the experiencer of all of it. Right now, I am experiencing the words on my computer screen, my fingers typing, the thoughts running through my mind, and a sense of being the one who is writing. These moments - when we think of ourselves, when we remember who we are - create the sense of self.

When we are engaged in an activity we forget ourselves, at least momentarily. During those moments we are just aware of what we are doing or our thoughts and feelings that are directly engaged in the task, without any thoughts about ourselves. Periodically, we remember ourselves. We imagine ourselves doing whatever we are doing. These moments give us a continuous sense of being the one who is doing. There are times when we are more lost in our activities than others. After remembering ourselves from a long period of being lost in some activity we will sometimes describe ourselves as having been deeply *into it*. These flow states, if they revolve around something we enjoy, are considered to be the source of happiness. It is when we lose our sense of self (often in an activity), that we feel free and happy. This is when we experience ourselves as being *in the flow,* or *in the moment.*

We assume that there is a real thing called our 'self' that is doing all the things that we see ourselves doing, but James wants us to question this assumption. What if there is no thing that we are? What if there are no things? What if reality is nothing but a flow of experience, and your sense of self is just an experienced moment of self-remembering? This shift in perspective is a huge leap, but it is one that can be very useful as a stepping stone to cosmic consciousness.

The point we are making in this chapter is that our experience of self-consciousness rests on an experience of being someone. The experience of being someone functions as a lens that shapes all of our experience. The sense of self takes our most intimate experience of being and projects out into the world as an imaginary entity. This projection of self creates an external vantage point from which to view both the world and ourselves. This ability to stand outside of our own experience creates the capacity for objectivity and abstract thought processes that dramatically expand what is possible in many ways.

Bucke holds a very optimistic view of self-consciousness. He sees it in a purely advantageous light. He was writing before two world wars and prior to any knowledge of widespread ecological collapse, and a host of other global problems that might make us question the ultimate value of the separate sense of self. Still, if we compare life today, as best we can imagine it, before the sense of self developed a million years ago, we cannot deny the magnitude of impact the sense of self had on human culture. Bucke wants us to appreciate the enormous magnitude of the leap that takes place from simple consciousness to self-consciousness that was made possible by the invention of language and the development and subsequent application of abstract reason. He does this because he wants us to have a sense of how vast the leap is from self-consciousness to cosmic consciousness.

You have a vast capacity for language and abstract reason and that allows you to understand what the sun is. You know that it's a star and you know what a star is and how it is different from the planet you live on. You know that you exist on the surface of a planet and you know when you should go out into the sun and when you should protect yourself from it. You understand why the sun is not visible at night and why it will come back each morning without fail. You know that sunny days will be warmer, you know that sunshine makes you happy, you know where on Earth it is most likely to be sunny at any particular time of year. Because you have language you are able to know so much about the sun and all of that understanding gives you a dramatically expanded range of possibilities to respond to, than say, a plant that might turn towards the light of the sun reflexively without having any choice in the matter. With the advent of self-consciousness a new universe of possibilities opens up. Similarly, with the advent of cosmic consciousness an equally dramatic expansion of possibility will open up. Those possibilities will not all be realized immediately, it might take generations of cosmically aware life to even begin to realize the full potential of that awakening. But the potential will be there, and in fact already is, as long as one human being reaches that epic next level of consciousness.

In the next chapter we will go into cosmic consciousness and what it is in detail, but before we move on, let's review what we have discovered about this first great leap in consciousness. Following in the footsteps laid out by Edward Carpenter and Richard Maurice Bucke we see consciousness in its most simple form as merely the capacity to react to stimuli. This minimal and completely unconscious ability to respond, gradually complexified. As creatures evolved to become more complex they began to exhibit more complex capacity for responding to stimuli. With the advent of the human form the ability to fashion crude hand tools represented a tremendous advancement in responsive capacity, but still we can imagine that self-consciousness had not yet evolved very much. Early cave paintings seem to indicate that human beings had developed the capacity to represent the world around them in pictures and had entered the road that would lead to abstract language. With the development of more sophisticated language human beings gained the capacity to imagine and represent themselves as another object in the world. This ability for self-objectification meant that they were now able to imagine the future and preemptively choose between different possible responses to circumstance to attain desired results. A period of dramatic acceleration of growth and possibility began through which the full potential of self-consciousness would gradually be realized.

It is not important that this picture of the evolution of consciousness is correct in the sense that it represents what really happened. I don't think it is possible to know precisely what really happened through the millions of years that life has developed on Earth. I do not even hold this picture of evolution as the only valuable one to consider and we look at a completely different view of evolution later. Still, there is a tremendous value to this sweeping picture of the evolution of consciousness and the most important insight that we can gain from it is the recognition that our experience of consciousness is not the only possible experience of consciousness. *In a profoundly fundamental way our experience of experiencing can change.*

Spiritual realization or enlightenment always pivots around a shift, not only in what we experience, but even more importantly, in how we experience. Enlightenment is not just another experience for us to have, it is a new way of experiencing. In this book I am equating cosmic consciousness with enlightenment, and the reasons why I am doing that will become clearer as our investigation moves forward, but what that means is that cosmic consciousness is not just an experience that we have, it is a new way of experiencing all together. I would ask you to contemplate this deeply. Contemplate and feel deeply into the possibility of discovering not just a new experience, but a new way of experiencing. It is not what you see in front of you that matters, it's where you are seeing from that makes all the difference.

SUMMARY OF EXERCISES

1. Take a moment to contemplate how much of your reality is conceptual. Imagine that you have no language at all. Look around you and imagine that you had no language, no words to represent anything. You simply have the pure sensual experience of seeing what is in front of you and no way of knowing what any of it is.

2. Ask yourself, who are you? Who is the person that responds to your name? Can you see that no answer you ever come up with will ever be more than abn aspect or part of you? Can you see that you will never be anything you can point to because you will always be the one pointing?

3. Contemplate and feel deeply into the possibility of discovering not just a new experience, but a new way of experiencing.

Describe in a notebook or journal about what you see in this investigation.

CHAPTER SIX

The Awakening of the Cosmos

"There must be awareness before there is change."

~ Eon

IF THERE IS ONLY ONE thing that you take away from the last chapter, I would want it to be that the miracle of cosmic consciousness is as far removed from our present condition of self-consciousness as that level of consciousness is from the most simple forms of consciousness. The paradox that you will need to embrace as our journey continues is that this new possibility is both completely different from our current experience, while at the same time being already here and present within us. We will use this chapter to set context for embracing that paradox, but before we do I need to address a potential objection that might be arising in your mind.

It may seem to you that although I promised that this book would offer practical guidance on the attainment of cosmic consciousness, it appears to contain a lot of information about a lot of things. You might make this objection on the grounds that the leap we are taking is into the mystery of the unknown and so nothing we know about it can be of any use. You would not be wrong in these objections, but not being wrong is not the same as being right.

Understanding is essential to awakening, even though nothing you understand and no insight you have can force an awakening upon you. If only it were that easy. If only there were an insight or an understanding that once shared would automatically lead to the awakening of anyone who learned it. All we would need to do is teach that insight or understanding and we would awaken the world. But it seems that no insight or understanding has that kind of consistent revelatory power. Of course there have been some people who were awakened by an insight or an understanding, but why they were awakened as a result of it and not everyone else who might have realized the same thing, is a mystery.

Someone once told me a story about a spiritual teacher who became enlightened watching the movie *Spartacus*. The film tells the story of a slave rebellion against the Roman empire led by Spartacus. The climactic scene depicts Spartacus and his army being confronted by the Roman representative after they are all captured by Rome. Rome is willing to spare the entire army if anyone will identify who Spartacus is. Spartacus himself stands up to identify himself, but before he can the person next to him stands and declares that he is Spartacus. Each member of the rebel army, one after another, stands to announce that they are Spartacus. During this moving display of unity, enlightenment dawned on the soon to be spiritual teacher, or so the story goes.

I wonder what insight the teacher gleaned from that scene. Perhaps he was just moved by the mass willingness to self-sacrifice rather than see their leader killed on their behalf. Or perhaps he saw in this dramatic act, a deeper recognition that each individual was being swept up in. Perhaps in that moment the entire army was seeing that they are all one, they actually were all Spartacus. They were not pretending to be Spartacus just to save their leader, they were expressing the deeper truth of oneness. Whatever the reason, this teacher was moved so deeply that his consciousness shifted into a new sphere. He saw the oneness of all things and from then on he had access to that profound view.

The film was directed by Stanely Kubrick and is generally considered a cinematic masterpiece. It has been seen by millions of people, but I have only ever heard of one that attained enlightenment through watching it. Why? Why did this one person experience such an extraordinary shift? What had prepared him for it?

It may be true that there is no insight that can awaken you, but it is also true that if an insight is to awaken you, you have to be ready for it to happen. Yes, of course there are stories of very rare individuals who experience the shift of awakening with no preparation at all, but if you look into the background of the person more deeply, you usually find that something had prepared them. Maybe it was life's hardship, or a deep inner yearning, but I have always found in each case that I have examined that something somehow had prepared them and made them open and receptive to the experience of awakening.

Understanding will not enlighten you, but understanding how the process of enlightenment takes place is almost always a necessary preparation that allows you to be open and receptive to the possibility. The miracle of enlightenment is always an accident. It always happens in a mysterious way without precedent or visible cause. It is a gift of grace. And yet, understanding and spiritual practice do seem to prepare the ground for that gift to be accepted upon.

I like to say that enlightenment is like falling asleep. You can't make yourself fall asleep, in fact, the harder you try, the more likely it is that you will be tormented by a sleepless night. At the same time, there are things that you can do to prepare yourself for sleep. You start slowing down, maybe you have a relaxing cup of tea, you turn off the lights and lay down. All of those things prepare you to be taken into sleep even though none of them cause you to fall asleep.

Spiritual study, contemplation, and practice are similar, they prepare you for the dawning of awakening, even though none of them are the cause of it happening. Another metaphor that I use is that awakening, enlightenment, cosmic consciousness, Self-realization, or whatever you want to call it, is like falling off the edge of a cliff. Spiritual understanding is part of what allows you to walk up to the edge ready to fall over. The study won't pull you across, but it gets you in the precarious place where you can be pulled into the process of awakening by the mysterious gravitational force of divinity.

Someone might still complain that all of this understanding is just useless information. It will need to be left behind in the end and so it is better not to pick it up in the first place. It is true, there is no understanding that can help you let go into the unknown so the complaint is not wrong, but that does not make it right. If we make such a statement, and it is one I have heard often, we will be missing something very important. Our conviction that no understanding can help us spiritually is itself an understanding that we are offering presumably to help someone spiritually. If you look deeply enough into your own experience you will see that it is inextricably infused with understanding. So deeply is reality interlaced with understanding that it is very hard for us to even distinguish between reality and our ideas about reality.

There are spiritual practices, like some forms of meditation, that are designed to bring us to a place of pure non-conceptual awareness. That means that our perception of reality has been completely cleared of any concepts. We are simply aware without any ideas about what it is that we are aware of. Anyone who is blessed with such an experience of bare attention will tell you that it is a very mysterious and magnificent event. On the one hand, you come out of that experience feeling that you have seen more clearly than you ever have before, at the same time you have no idea what you saw and so it feels as if you saw nothing at all. You remember the experience as one of vivid luminosity, but you can't remember anything about it. In this experience we see how deeply conceptual our normal experience of reality is. From the surface all the way through to the depths of our perception there are concepts interwoven with sensation creating what we imagine to be real.

Cosmic consciousness is real, it is possible for you to attain, and there are ways to prepare for it that will invite it into your life. Please consider what you just read. Look at each of the three parts of that statement. Do you believe each of them to be true? An important part of your preparation for cosmic consciousness is believing without doubt that cosmic consciousness is real, that it is possible for you to attain, and that you can prepare for it in ways that will invite it into your life. Thank you for being patient and staying with me as I lay out what I believe is crucial understanding in preparation for the miracle of cosmic consciousness. I promise not to share more than I think is necessary, and to be as concise and illuminating as I can be in doing so.

I have no doubt about the reality of cosmic consciousness because I have experienced it. As I already described I experienced an expansion into my cosmic self during a meditation retreat. This was a dramatic and unforgettable experience. This, along with other spiritual openings that I have had, removed any fear of death because I became aware that I existed as pure consciousness before I was born and will continue to exist in that form after this body ceases to function. It left me doubtless about the reality of oneness, not just in the sense that all things are interconnected, which is true, but in the more profound sense that everything is made of consciousness. Consciousness is all there is. Some would disagree with me on this, and I could certainly be wrong, but the fact that I could be wrong on this point makes me no less convinced of it. I am certain about this and the very real possibility of being mistaken doesn't make me less convinced. If I become convinced tomorrow that something else is true, I will change. I am not committed to holding onto the idea of oneness as a fact. I am simply utterly convinced of the reality or it.

This book is very special to me because I believe that articulating, living and sharing cosmic consciousness is my life's work. I believe it is what I was born for. When I experienced an awakening to cosmic consciousness on retreat I was thirty nine years old. I had been part of an intensely focused spiritual practice community for nearly ten years and during that time all of my life's energy was focused on spiritual study, contemplation and practice. I also mentioned how after that experience I remembered that I had regularly stretched into my cosmic being as a small child. After my reawakening, I remembered my early spiritual experiences vividly, but until that moment I had forgotten about them completely. Once I remembered those early experiences my whole life made sense.

To put it briefly, as a child I had a technique that consistently guided the expansion of my being into its cosmic proportions. I would stare deeply into my own eyes in a mirror and relax into the sense of expansion. I would blow up until my head went through the roof of the house, then way up high into the sky, then into outer space until the entire universe was my body. At that point I would have the most wonderful feeling of love and belonging. I would know that this was my home and I would relax down to the core of my being. I was only about three years old, I am sure I didn't fully understand what I was experiencing. I just loved it and there was a sense that I was returning back to where I came from before I was born. After my adult experience of cosmic consciousness I remembered clearly these early journeys, and I remembered the day I looked into my eyes and couldn't do it anymore. I felt trapped, sad and afraid. I had no way back now. I became resigned to the fact that I was just going to have to find a way to be here as comfortably as I could.

I don't have any idea when I might have forgotten about these experiences, but certainly by the time I was about seven they were long gone. At that age I became obsessed with trying to escape my mind. I was certain that just beyond the never ending succession of thoughts there was another universe waiting for me. A few years later I would lie on my back on summer afternoons or evenings until I felt a thrilling emotional elation at the recognition of how vast the universe was and how small I was resting on the surface of this planet. When I was older still

I experimented with mind altering drugs, then meditation and spiritual practices. And I was still on this journey when I met the teacher whose community I would join and spend the next twenty years in.

When I met my former teacher I was married to a wonderful woman, owned a beautiful house and had a good paying career as an engineer. After meeting my teacher I left it all to join a radical, and some would say abusive, spiritual community. My first step on that journey was to move into the studio apartment owned by another student. I was twenty nine years old, she was sixty. I slept on her floor. I would wake up at night thinking about my ex-wife and the beautiful house that I had just walked away from and wonder if I was crazy.

I knew why I had left, but it sometimes didn't make sense to me. What had motivated such a dramatic change were two mind-blowing experiences of higher consciousness that I had in the presence of my teacher. As a result of these openings I experienced what I could call full body transparency. I could see through my own body and everyone else's. I could read other people's minds and know what they were going to say before they would say it. I was beginning to understand everything that I had ever heard from any of the many spiritual books I'd read and it all seemed like the obvious truth of my current experience. The most powerful of these experiences lasted for months. During that time I felt like I was as light as a feather, floating above the ground all the time. And I seemed to be connected to a supercharge of energy that flooded my system. I knew that these experiences were the reason I had left my perfectly good life. That was the reason, but it still didn't seem like a satisfactory explanation to me. I could understand that the experiences were powerful, but it still seemed out of character for me to give up my entire life because of them.

A little of my background might help explain my confusion. I came from a second generation Portuguese American family and the idea of leaving both my wife and my career were unthinkable to me until I did them. It was always a mystery how I had found the motivation and the courage to step out of my life. After remembering my earliest experiences of cosmic consciousness it all made so much sense. Ever since I was a young child I had a feeling that I didn't belong in this world. I felt like an alien who had arrived here from another planet. I wasn't interested in what other kids found fascinating. I didn't understand why adults were doing what they were doing. Nothing made sense to me. Now I know why.

The experiences I had when I met my former teacher must have unconsciously convinced me that I had found a way home, back to the cosmic sense of love and belonging that I had known as a child. It was the loss of my capacity to experience cosmic consciousness that left me feeling that I didn't belong. Discovering a potential way back to that expansive state was worth everything I had to give. It wasn't easy to do, but it was worth giving up the life I had for the chance to find a way back to my cosmic self. The experience I had on retreat was the payoff. I had returned to my true home. That was not the only powerful experience I had on that retreat, but it was one of the most powerful and I can honestly say that the person who completed that retreat was not the same person who entered it and he never would be again.

I wanted to share that story because I believe that it is all of our story. As I said at the beginning of this book, my opinion is that the only reason you felt compelled to read this book is because you have already experienced cosmic consciousness. You may remember it, you may be about to remember it, or you may never remember it. It doesn't matter. I feel certain that cosmic consciousness is already yours. Think about your spiritual life. Doesn't it make much more sense if you assume that you had an experience of cosmic consciousness at some early point that you no longer remember? Don't your consistent spiritual choices make more sense that way? The more you think about your life this way the more sense it will make. It will seem more and more obvious that you must have had an early experience of cosmic consciousness that has been the source of your spiritual passion ever since.

I didn't remember my own early experiences of cosmic consciousness until after I experienced it again decades later as an adult on a meditation retreat. At the time that I had that experience on retreat, I was not familiar with the phrase cosmic consciousness and I had never heard of Richard Maurice Bucke or Edward Carpenter. I wouldn't find out about all that until a few years later.

After that retreat I started to emerge as a prominent member of my spiritual community. I became my teacher's personal assistant, I started to develop programs of study around his teaching, and I began to teach myself. My teacher had experienced a powerful awakening with a teacher of Advaita Vedanta, but by the time I had met him he was already teaching an early form of what he called evolutionary enlightenment. I developed a five week course to share the basics of that teaching and it was in one of my early classes that I first remember hearing about cosmic consciousness and Richard Maurice Bucke.

The fourth session of the course was my favorite to teach because it shared in the most condensed possible form, the essence of evolutionary enlightenment. I would speak about the evolutionary process from an anthropocentric point of view.

The class would end with a guided contemplation. I asked everyone to imagine that they were the consciousness of the universe, but before the universe had come into existence. You can do it right now. Imagine that you are pure consciousness, but with nothing yet to be conscious of. You are really just the potential to be conscious because you won't become conscious until there is something to be conscious of. That pure consciousness is almost totally empty. There is almost nothing at all there, but there must have been something that emerged to get the whole process started. Imagine that what emerged in the emptiness of pure consciousness was nothing but a mysterious urge, a pull, a longing, a desire. For what? To know, to feel, to experience, to exist. There is a longing to manifest in a form that can be known. Imagine that for untold eons of time that is all there was, the potential to know and the desire to know, but so far nothing in existence that could be known. Then something happened. Something appeared. A particle, an energy. Something tiny, barely noticeable, but from your point of view it was immense. The difference between having nothing to experience and having something to experience is vast even if the something is itself barely noticeable. You finally have something to know. Maybe it is just a single particle, but it is something. Eons more time passes and all you have is that one particle to know, until another particle appears. Now you have two. It is wonderful.

Slowly more and more particles appear, and more energies that connect them. Finally stars appear and planets and after an incredible amount of time, life appears, simple single cells of living matter, … life! More time passes and eventually there are complex plants and then animals. The plants and animals begin to respond to their environment. They are alive in a complex way. It is wonderful. More and more variations appear. The world is filling up with life. Then something amazing happens and one of those life forms recognizes themselves to be alive and conscious. This life form is self-conscious. This is new. This is exciting. It is a miracle. Somehow a life form developed the capacity to recognize itself and you know that the consciousness it has to recognize itself with, is yours. That life form does not have its own consciousness separate from you. Its consciousness is an extension of you. You are the source of consciousness after all. The members of this species think that they are the source of their own consciousness. They believe it is being generated within them, probably in their brains. They believe they are separate living entities, completely isolated from one another and from you, the source of all consciousness.

This mistaken identity propagates through generations until something miraculous happens. Some of the self-conscious beings look inside with enough focus and humility to begin to open to an unimaginable possibility. They look inward and they see you, their true source. They suddenly know that they are one with you. They see that their consciousness is all coming from the same source, you. They have awakened from the dream of isolation and separation into the reality of unity and oneness. But at this same moment, at the same time that the first individuals looked inside to find their own source, something happened to you as well. Suddenly you were not just seeing their awakening from the outside. Suddenly, in a rush of energetic flow, you found yourself, the very source of universal consciousness, experiencing through them. You could see through their eyes, could think using their mind, feel with their heart. You, the source of consciousness, was finally having a lived, manifest, human experience. You had created a universe and you had found your way inside. These individuals, the ones who had awakened to the reality of you, the ones who you were now flowing through, these individuals were different. They were seeing things in a completely new way, thinking things that were not possible to think before, and doing things that would previously have been unimaginable. And as they embraced this new way of being more and more deeply the distinction between the individual awareness and the universal source of awareness began to disappear and these seemingly isolated beings began to realize that they were you.

As I finished this guided contemplation. One of the students in the class shouted out, "Oh my god! Maurice Bucke said all that over a hundred years ago!" He was not trying to minimize what I had just shared, in fact he loved it. He was just thrilled to hear what sounded to him like such a clear and authentic expression of cosmic consciousness. He was pleased that I knew nothing of Bucke. He enjoyed sharing with me what he knew and suggested very emphatically that I buy a copy of the book right away, which I did.

As I have looked at my own life history in light of these early childhood experiences more and more pieces have fallen into place. One of those pieces only clicked into place for me a few years ago. My very first spiritual teacher was Captain Marvel. Having remembered my early childhood experiences I began to see an unconscious throughline that was persistently operating during my entire life. I believe if you are here reading this book, and you are, there is a similar organizing principle at work in your life. Some experience, or experiences that you had early in this life or in some previous one have exerted a pull on you that has led you right here to this book. As you continue to read this book, hold your heart in a gentle open stance, that means be curious about what spiritual experiences might be alive and operating in you that you don't remember.

When my early memories were reawakened I saw my life through a different lens. Examined as a quest to find my way back to my spiritual home, I could see so many things that had seemed random or inconsequential suddenly seem relevant and mysteriously deliberate. One of the elements that fell into a new place of prominence in revisualizing my spiritual history was my boyhood love of Captain Marvel comics.

Captain Marvel was a Marvel comics title that was written and drawn by Jim Starlin during the years that I was reading them. Captain Marvel was my first favorite superhero and he is known as "the most cosmic superhero of all." That doesn't seem random at all. Captain Marvel's primary superpower was cosmic awareness. Of course he was my favorite. When he would go into a state of cosmic awareness Starlin would draw his face close up and over a few frames in the comic book, his facial features would gradually dissolve away and be replaced with a view of the vast and starry cosmos. It was as if his face had become an open portal to the entire universe. In this state, Captain Marvel had access to all knowledge.

Some time after the experience I had on retreat I saw an image of Captain Marvel in the state of cosmic awareness. I remembered how I loved those comics and would spend hours drawing or tracing Captain Marvel's face full of stars. A new connection was made in my mind. Of course I had fallen in love with a character who so obviously shared my cosmic origin. At a later point I went back and read the comics that had fascinated me as a boy. I was amazed at what I found.

There is a long storyline that took place over many monthly issues that I remember reading when I was about eight years old. The background of the story is that Captain Marvel has reached the limits of his powers. He is a warrior from an alien world, and although his aims are good, his means are still violent. He is the self-proclaimed protector of Earth, but he finds that he is not powerful enough to defeat his greatest foe, Thanos. At a low point in his quest, Captain Marvel is brought into a mysterious dimension called the Negative Zone, which is described as being neither here, nor there, nor anywhere in between. In this non-place he meets a powerful godlike being called Eon.

Eon has summoned Captain Marvel to the Negative Zone to tell him that he can never be victorious the way he is operating. He cannot protect Earth as a warrior, and so he must transform. Captain Marvel then embarks upon a spiritual training with Eon's guidance that finally leads to the attainment of his true superpower, cosmic awareness.

As part of his training Captain Marvel must face death and conquer his fear by realizing that death is not an ending, but a change and a new beginning. Only by facing death can he discover that true life is freedom, but the final transformation he seeks cannot occur unless he authentically wants it to happen. Once he truly desires it, the change will happen immediately and inevitably.

His spiritual work begins with a battle against the Ravengers. These are the false beliefs and negative tendencies like vanity, greed and pride, that destroy our dreams before we can realize them. After a long and arduous battle has been won, Captain Marvel is at the doorstep of realization, but he still must SEE.

Having defeated his inner demons, he gazes upon the strange face of Eon floating in the non-space of the Negative Zone. Eon's head has one large eye that he calls his Soul Eye, but it could be the third eye of Hindu mysticism. Captain Marvel must find the courage to stare into the Soul Eye until the final vestiges of negativity have been eclipsed by a direct vision of reality as it is. His warrior spirit must die, but the change cannot be forced from the outside, it must come from within. When the transformation is complete, our hero is blessed with the true sight of cosmic consciousness.

There is no way, after having remembered my childhood experiences, that I could see my love for Captain Marvel as a random coincidence. Of course there are still a number of ways that we could interpret the connection between my love for these comics and my earlier experiences of cosmic consciousness.

In our secular world that believes in the unconscious power of psychology, but not so much in the mysterious powers of mysticism, we might see my love of Captain Marvel as the cause of my later experience of cosmic consciousness. Perhaps I was first captivated by the comic book and my later spiritual experience was shaped by my early reading about the superpower of cosmic awareness. The memories of my childhood experiences of cosmic consciousness might simply have been invented by my unconscious mind. This might seem like a plausible explanation to some people, but it doesn't feel at all accurate to me.

We could also adopt an equally personal, but far more mystical interpretation by assuming that my early forgotten experiences of cosmic consciousness were the reason why I loved Captain Marvel in the first place. This seems far more likely to me. I would also note that after Captain Marvel, the two heroes I loved the most were Dr. Strange the spiritual magician who learned the mystical arts from a master in Tibet, and the Vision, another alien being from another world who had profound powers of omniscient awareness. It seems very likely to me that I gravitated toward these characters over much more popular superheroes because they all linked to my early awakening experiences.

There is yet another way that these experiences can be interpreted and it is the way I resonate with the most. It could be that cosmic consciousness is awakening not just in me, or you, or anyone else, but in this world. There is an awakening to a new level of consciousness that is occurring and has been occurring for a long time. Our experiences of cosmic consciousness are not so much personal experiences as they are moments when we touch into the awakening that is occurring on this planet. I believe this is the most accurate way for me to interpret my experience, and as anyone who has read my book *The Path of Spiritual Breakthrough* will know, I believe that how we interpret our spiritual breakthrough experiences is just as important as having them.

When you awaken to cosmic consciousness, part of what you awaken to is the fact that consciousness is universal, not personal. Yes, you have a personal and totally unique experience of consciousness, but the source of that consciousness is universal. The consciousness that any of us experience is coming from the same source. Some of us are more sensitive to the awakened energy of cosmic consciousness. We feel the energy of the awakening and it ignites an experience in our being, but what we are feeling is an awakening that is happening in consciousness. It is one of many experiences that exist in consciousness, like there are many sounds in an orchestra. If you listen to a symphony with a well trained ear, you can hear all of the different instruments in a way that the untrained ear cannot distinguish. The wine connoisseur can taste individual flavors in a wine that most of us miss. Those of us who have a sensitivity to cosmic consciousness are able to feel that experience within the symphony of consciousness. Our spiritual practice helps us to gain greater spiritual expertise so we are better able to focus on that experience and ignore other elements of consciousness that might compete for our attention.

There is an awakening of cosmic consciousness happening. It is not happening in individuals, although it is experienced by individuals. It is an awakening in consciousness. What we will see as we continue our inquiry is that it might be more useful to think of cosmic consciousness as the cosmos awakening to itself through you, rather than you awakening to your cosmic being. Both of those interpretations are true, but they unlock different potentials within us and so they must both be embraced and worked with.

I want to tell you a little story to help make my point clear. I once had the opportunity to meet the famous hippie folk singer Arlo Guthrie. I found him to be a beautiful man. He was a deep spiritual practitioner working within a Hindu context and he exuded a vivacious character and love of life. He felt awake and alive to me. During the short time that we spent together there was one question I wanted to ask, *what were the sixties really like?* I felt it was kind of a silly question, too general and vague to really be answered, but I couldn't help myself and I asked it anyway. His answer was beautiful.

If you don't know Arlo Guthrie he was an icon of the counterculture. His song *Alice's Restaurant* is an ode to a renovated church where hippies traveling between Boston and New York could always find a place to sleep and a hot spaghetti dinner. The song captures the spirit and ideals of the time and continues to be regularly played on the American Thanksgiving holiday.

When I asked Arlo what the sixties were really like, his eyes sparkled and a broad smile appeared on his face. Clearly he was feeling it. He bent down towards the ground and then stood up making a big sweeping gesture over his head and said, "Oh man!

It was rising up out of the Earth and we were just catching the wave!" He didn't say anything more about it. He didn't have to. His eyes, his smile, his sweeping gesture and that short statement had already communicated everything I could have hoped for.

Many of those who participated in the sixties counterculture movement felt that they were participating in the emergence of something bigger than they were. They were catching a wave of rising consciousness. They were feeling it personally and were being transformed by it, and it was a movement of energy that was arising out of the Earth. It was an expansion of consciousness, not any individual's consciousness, but the conscious source that we all share. Those who felt the emergence and engaged with it were fueling its continued growth, and they knew it was bigger than them.

Jim Starlin, the artist and author of Captain Marvel, was also part of that counterculture emergence. As the sixties aged into the seventies the artists at Marvel Comics who had created such classics as Spiderman, the Hulk, and Captain America were aging too. A new group of artists began to occupy the drawing tables and desks at Marvel Comics. They, like Jim Starlin, were a new generation. They were young, they were vietnam vets, they were hippies, they took acid, and they spent their breaks from work out on the balcony smoking dope. They were reading Carlos Castaneda, H. P. Lovecraft, and books on Zen Buddhism and Hindu philosophy. They were steeped in new ideas and new ways of thinking and all of that was finding its way into the stories they wrote for comics.

And there was me at age eight or nine or ten, reading about eastern philosophy and cosmic consciousness without any idea about what it was or where it came from. To me they were just comics and the stories were just stories. Every summer my father would insist that I read ten books cover to cover, I would beg that at least five of them could be comics. Little did he know that he was introducing me to Eastern ideas of enlightenment that would change my life. During those summer months as I followed the adventure of Captain Marvel, my personal life's story intersected with a larger cultural story. I was encountering an awakening of consciousness that Jim Starlin and his friends were reading in some of the same books that I would fall in love with a decade later.

I want to encourage you to think about cosmic consciousness, not only as a personal experience that you can have, but as a wave of higher psychic potentials that are erupting out of the universe itself. Yes, we are becoming cosmically aware, like Captain Marvel did, but equally and perhaps more importantly, the cosmos itself is becoming aware through us. I was born with a connection to my celestial home that I lost contact with. Then I encountered ideas about that home in comic books. I devoured those books, I spent hours tracing the illustrations in them. My engagement with those comic books was an early form of my spiritual practice. I had encountered a cultural movement, a cosmic wave and I wanted to ride it.

My friend and colleague Jeffrey Kripal of Rice University spends a great deal of his academic career studying how paranormal ideas can be found in the images, music, writing and films of popular culture. In his amazing book *Mutants and Mystics* he writes about how we encounter evolving trends in consciousness on two levels, as mythical stories about the extraordinary, and as our own extraordinary paranormal and spiritual experiences. He also explains how neither of these is necessarily the cause of the other. In fact, each of them creates the other in a strange loop of causality. Jim Starlin read about strange phenomena and likely experienced them. Whatever he learned and experienced became part of the comics he was writing, which I then read. My childhood experiences allowed me to recognize what Starlin was writing, even if I wasn't consciously aware of it. I was compelled to study more until decades later, while living in a spiritual community and sitting on a meditation cushion, I experienced cosmic consciousness as an adult. Now I write books and novels in which I can express everything that I have experienced and you are reading one of them. Your own deeper experiences of cosmic consciousness made you interested in reading this book and they allow you to see the underlying picture I am trying to paint here. You inevitably will share whatever inspires you with others in some way or another. The looping goes on and on. Cultural elements affect individuals and individual experiences become new cultural elements.

Consciousness and culture create each other and we are swept along a river of individual and collective experience. If we want to think about this in terms of transmission we could say that Jim Starlin was getting a transmission from his reading and whatever experiences he was having. I was getting a transmission of at least the idea of cosmic consciousness from him. You cannot separate your own experience of consciousness from the collective consciousness that you are embedded in. You may have particular sensitivities to certain aspects of the collective, but you are entangled with it. I believe, and we will explore later in this book, that we cannot pursue cosmic consciousness entirely on our own, and I mean that literally, we can't, because we are already part of the wider collective in which the experience of cosmic consciousness is alive.

Before this chapter comes to an end I want to take you even further out than this. In one of our conversations, Jeffrey Kripal described something to me that I will never forget. He told me that one of his mentors at the University of Chicago had been Dr. Culianu, who had an amazing theory about the history of religion. He believed that the entire history of religion, from the beginning to now and long into the future, was being caused by a higher dimensional being that was passing through our three-dimensional reality. As the vital and psychic energy of this unimaginable being passes through our reality, which it would do across all of our time simultaneously, individual human beings, and perhaps some members of other species, would be infused with the higher consciousness of this being. These infusions of higher being are the cause of our spiritual experiences.

I am not presenting you with that wonderful idea so that you can decide if it is true, it is not generally useful to approach such a radical idea from the standpoint of validating it. Instead, I ask you to consider what aspects of that idea might be true? Or put another way, what aspects of reality might be revealed to us if we take that idea seriously?

I can easily embrace the idea that my spiritual experiences emerged from a higher dimension. That is often exactly how it feels to have a breakthrough. It starts small and then seems to seep into your entire being. If I think of some of my most profound experiences I can feel them this way. Perhaps my experience of cosmic consciousness was me coming into contact with the consciousness of being from another dimension. I have talked with Jeffrey Kripal about how our non-ordinary experiences often feel as if they were looking for us, as we were looking for them. In his book *Authors of the Impossible* he speaks about how our paranormal experiences are messengers carrying messages. There is something that wants to be communicated through these events. These experiences want to be known as much as we want to know them.

I want you to think about any paranormal or spiritual experiences that you've had, imagining that they are entities that are trying to communicate something important to you. See how it changes your memory of the experience by giving the experience a more active role in generating the event that occurred. If we only see our spiritual experiences as inner events that we have, we might be missing something. Perhaps they are alive and wanting to be experienced.

We can think of cosmic consciousness as an experience that we have, but if we do, it easily becomes all about us. I don't believe that way of thinking unlocks the deeper potentials of the experience. I believe that it is more powerful to realize that the universe itself is waking up through you. When you experience that cosmic being, maybe it is not you experiencing your cosmic self, maybe it is the cosmos, which is also you, waking up to its own existence. In that exalted state of universal grandeur, we realize that we are the cosmos. I am that. If you have had even a glimpse of cosmic consciousness, or if you have one while reading this book, please contemplate the possibility that it was not you waking up to a higher state of consciousness, it was the source of consciousness itself gaining access to your mind and body and seeing itself through a human being.

During the retreat in which the experience of cosmic consciousness returned to me, I kept a journal. As I began to realize that it was not me that was awakening, it was the universe herself waking up through me, I would write questions to contemplate the magnificent future I was feeling. Once the cosmos becomes fully awakened in human form, once all human beings are animated by her vast consciousness and supreme love, what will happen? What will a truly cosmic conscious world look like? If you feel excitement at what might be possible when a global transformation to cosmic consciousness happens, you will be feeling the same thrill that was driving Edward Carpenter, Richard Maurice Bucke and so many other spiritually inspired souls. Now it is time for us to leave this chapter and consider more fully the implications of higher dimensions of reality.

SUMMARY OF EXERCISES

Think about any paranormal or spiritual experiences that you've had and imagine that it was actually a living entity that came to you to communicate something important. How does that perspective change your memory of the event? What do you think the message of that experience was? Describe in a notebook or journal about what you see in this investigation.

CHAPTER SEVEN

The Fourth-Dimension and Creative Illumination

"One of these days we'll understand the fundamental thing that's given us space in the first place and dimensions of space in particular."

~ Lisa Randall, American physicist

I WOULDN'T BLAME YOU IF you were a bit skeptical of my claims that this would be a practical guide to cosmic consciousness. After all, how practical can you be about something like cosmic consciousness? I want to keep reassuring you that my intention is that this book be a guide into the glorious vision of all-inclusive oneness that is cosmic consciousness. And I keep repeating that because part of what makes this a practical guide is your relating to it as one. What it means to be practical about a subject like this, is not the same as what it means to be practical about baking a cake or building a house. This isn't a recipe book and I can't give you a blueprint. You won't find the eight steps to cosmic awareness here, because there are no steps that can be described and followed to where this book is pointing.

What you will find is clear and simple descriptions and explanations of what I believe is the essential understanding that will bring you to the very edge of a miracle. You will also find guidance for spiritual practices that are equally essential for the journey. You will need to work with what is here, do the practices and contemplations, and stretch your mind to imagine the unimaginable. In the last chapter we explored a vision of the evolution of consciousness. Making the effort to see your current consciousness as part of an evolutionary unfolding helps create the sense of scale that creates the space and inner fluidity that is essential for the shift that we are pursuing. The self-consciousness experience you have right now was born as part of the conceptual reality that is infused with language and characterized by the simultaneous awareness of both yourself and the world outside yourself. Seeing this as a recent development in the vast history of cosmic evolution helps us open to the enormous magnitude and unimaginable novelty of the new consciousness.

This evolutionary context for enlightenment was part of what inspired me enough to leave my wife and career and join a spiritual community. For years I taught an evolutionary view of enlightenment and shared my passion for the recognition that we were all riding the wave of cosmic unfolding. When I was teaching about or contemplating the unimaginable trajectory of evolution, I would often find myself swept up into an unimaginable shift in awareness. I would see how unimaginably immense the universe was, not just in terms of space as I lay in the grass on warm summer nights, but also in relation to the passing of time. My perspective would shift. I would continue to be aware of everything around me, including my body and mind, but I was no longer in the familiar world of localized time and space. In these moments my entire experience of reality, the entire three-dimensional world and everything in it throughout all of time, would become paper thin in a way that I cannot describe. It was as if three dimensions had collapsed into two and my entire experience of reality had become a flat surface that was speeding along through space like the windshield of an automobile moving at an impossible speed. The entire three-dimensional reality that was the only universe I had ever known was a windshield moving at light speed, evolving as it went. The direction that the windshield traveled in could not be imagined because it was outside of space and time. And I was not a person existing like a speck of dust on that windshield; I was the entire windshield. I am the cosmos and the cosmos is a paper three-dimensional windshield hurtling through higher dimensional reality shifting, changing and evolving as it goes.

In these miraculous moments my former experience of myself did not disappear. It didn't even change. It was just seen from a much bigger context. The experience of being Jeff, who was a human being living on the spherical surface of a planet called Earth with all of its beauty and richness intact, was now seen as part of the leading edge of the universal windshield traveling in a direction that was beyond my ability to understand. I would stand in front of the people in my classes, look out at their faces and exclaim that I and we are the leading edge of the universe evolving. I would feel it with every cell of my being. I would see in a way that cannot be described in words, how the entirety of the experience that is happening right now - my experience of talking - everyone else's experience of listening - and all of the other experiences that anyone anywhere was having were all part of the leading edge of the evolutionary process. That vision was, and continues to be, deeply real to me.

We already saw how the miracle of self-conscious awareness was made possible by the advent of language. The question that naturally raises is, what advancement in human capacity makes cosmic consciousness possible. In this chapter I will share my conviction that what makes cosmic consciousness possible is the development of multi-dimensional awareness. As long as our perceptual ability remains rigidly limited to the three-dimensions of space and time that we are familiar with, we will not have the mental flexibility to be carried off into the miracle of cosmic consciousness. The awakening that we seek requires that we expand beyond ourselves. Our earlier contemplation of the field of consciousness and the art of self-forgetting are two ways that we can liberate ourselves, ever so slightly, from the limits of our ordinary perceptual reality. In this chapter we will enter an inquiry into higher dimensional reality directly and discover that we are not the first to apply those realities to the experience of cosmic consciousness.

The act of writing a book like this is a spiritual practice and mystical process. I tend to work spontaneously. I have very little plan for the book beyond a vague sense of progression that seems to be necessary at the start even though it seldom lasts throughout the duration of the process. The book that emerges at the end of the writing process is always a mystery. I believe that the creation of art is always a mystical event. An artist does not work like a contractor taking plans and instructions and manifesting them as a building. An artist approaches the work the way you would approach the edge of a diving board before diving in. Any plans the artist might have brought with them to the edge quickly flutter away in the wind as the gravity of creation takes over. I fall into my art. Communicating with it as we both move according to a force that neither of us controls. I begin to type some thoughts, the thoughts on the page speak to me, telling me what to type next. Those next words open new passage ways forward. We tumble together, the book and I, toward completion.

It is not only the process of writing that is spontaneous for me. The process of research is also a spontaneous event. I know that many authors would tend to want to research first and write later. I do both at the same time. I start writing and then the writing directs me to things I must learn more about. I read about those things, or talk to people that know about them, and return to the writing ready to show the fruits of my research to the book. I write until the book asks for more research and I go again into a discovery mode. What is amazing to me is how perfectly the book researches itself through me. There is a book that wants to be written. Part of it can simply be written from my existing experience, but part of it must be written using ideas that I find somewhere else. The book tells me exactly what is necessary.

Who is creating this book then? Am I writing it? Is the book writing itself? Or is the universe the true author? I believe that the universe is the true author, I am the writing instrument. The universe is using me to write this book. I am surrendering to a process that wants to happen. That is why for me, writing is a mystical event and a spiritual practice. It is an act of surrender to a process that wants to happen. Jeff sometimes gets nervous, he believes he doesn't have anything more to say. He worries that the book is not going anywhere. But Jeff is only nervous in those moments when he forgets that he is not writing the book. The universe is. This same idea can be applied to all of our lives. Who is living your life? You are taught that you are, but in the experience of cosmic consciousness, you realize that you are being lived. Something is living through you. Yes you make decisions, have preferences, and take actions, but all of that, as wonderful as it is, is only possible because you are alive and living. You are making decisions and acting, but that is all happening in the thinnest outer edge of life. Living is what gets you to the place where decisions and actions can happen. You are not doing the living. If I wasn't already living, I wouldn't have the merest possibility of giving birth to myself. The more deeply you see that everything you commonly call life is really being lived and supported by something much bigger than you, the more you become aware of the cosmic oneness that includes everything.

The experience of my life as being lived from and by a higher source and riding at the very edge of evolution was one of the deepest and most profound revelations that has shaped who I am and what I do. At the same time, I have for some time also felt that the evolutionary view, as powerful and valuable as it is, can also be misleading. A few weeks ago I was guided to do research for this book and specifically to take another look at the delightful book about the fourth dimension called *Flatland* by Edwin Abott. That led me to read the ideas of Charles Howard Hinton about the fourth dimension. And that led me to a wonderful book called *Tertium Organum* by P. D. Ouspensky. I have been inhaling Ouspensky's book as well as other biographical information about him. Sometimes in the unpredictable process of researching for a particular book, I find something that is so perfect on so many levels, not just for that book, but for me, that I cannot do more than be grateful for whatever spirit it is that guides me. *Tertium Organum* is one of those miraculous finds that happened at exactly the right time for reasons beyond what I know.

Ouspensky had already read both Edward Carpenter and Richard Maurice Bucke when he wrote *Tertium Organum*, and he was very much in agreement with most of the ways that the idea of cosmic consciousness had been developed by them. He was not entirely onboard, however, especially with some of Bucke's conclusions. I was amazed to find so many of my misgivings about an exclusively evolutionary context for awakening expressed in Ouspensky's writing. Before reading his book I had never looked deeply into his work, although it was certainly part of the ecology of ideas that I had been living in for decades.

P. D. Ouspensky was a Russian philosopher and mystic who is best known as the chief disciple and foremost spokesperson of the Russian spiritual teacher George Ivanovich Gurdjieff. As I read more about Ouspensky I discovered that he was a well known lecturer and philosopher in his own right before meeting Gurdjieff. He had already written and published *Tertium Organum* and was recognized by many as a true mystic. He met Gurdjieff and fell in love with his system of teaching. Ouspensky's later book *In Search of the Miraculous*, is often spoken of as the clearest and most accessible presentation of Gurdjieff's vast body of work. Some, like Ouspensky's biographer Colin Wilson, would say that meeting Gurdjieff was the worst thing that could have happened to Ouspensky because it distracted him from his earlier work which might have developed into a system more powerful than his teacher's. I don't feel qualified to have an opinion about that, but I can say that *Tertium Organum*, as difficult a read as it can be, hit me like a thunderbolt.

Ouspensky articulates what he sees as the shortcomings of Bucke's presentation of cosmic consciousness, and as I said, his criticisms exactly correspond to my own. Cosmic consciousness, when it is too tightly bound to the idea of evolution lacks a certain higher dimensionality. As utterly enthusiastic as I was about evolutionary spirituality, I also saw that it was too easy for it to be seen as something much less profound than it was. To be fair, this is not just a problem with evolutionary forms of spirituality, it is true of any enlightenment teaching. Teachings of that which is beyond understanding are always in danger of being misunderstood. There will always be a tendency for even the sinere aspirant to grasp at what can be seen and understood while missing the vast invisible that is the true heart of the matter.

I am presenting what I see as potential pitfalls of evolutionary forms of spirituality, but these are not inherent to that view. Most people I know who teach this powerful form of spiritual work do their best to avoid the pitfalls. The challenge is not ultimately tied to evolutionary spirituality, but with the search for the miraculous in general. We are pursuing something that is mysterious and far removed from our current experience and it is very difficult for us not to reduce it to something that feels intelligible to us. Of course any spiritual path will lend itself more to certain pitfalls than others. In fact, new spiritual paths often emerge as a correction to the pitfalls of a previous one, those attempts to correct will inevitably have their own blindspots and pitfalls and new paths will be developed to address those. There is no way to completely mitigate the risk of spiritual pursuit.

One of the hazards that evolutionary forms of spirituality are particularly susceptible to is the creation of false hierarchies. If the human experience of self-consciousness is the leading edge of the evolutionary process isn't it better than previous forms of consciousness? Are humans really a higher form of life on the planet? The evolutionary view, as powerful as it can be, can be dangerous if it creates a false sense of superiority. Anytime we see some people, or cultures, or species as more evolved than others, we find ourselves navigating treacherous waters. How can we gain the benefit of the expanded sense of reality that the evolutionary view brings without creating false hierarchical structures?

What I was most delighted to find in Ouspensky's book is that he had come to the same conclusion that I had as to what a better context for cosmic consciousness might be. In addition to thinking in terms of the evolution of consciousness, I want to suggest that you think in terms of the expansion of consciousness into greater dimensionality. This shift in context will help us hold both the true depth of the transformation we are exploring, while avoiding some of the limitations of a view that is overly wedded to development that occurs along the arrow of time. Ouspensky comes to this conclusion along a path similar to the one that I had followed, although he was working a century earlier. The path runs through the idea of the fourth dimension as presented by Edwin Abott and C. H. Hinton in their writings.

Edwin Abbott's little book *Flatland*, published in 1884 presents a humorous story that takes place in a world that is limited to only two dimensions. It is a flat world that is simply a plane, like the flat surface of a piece of paper stretched infinitely in two directions. The main character of the story is A Square. His world is populated by polygons, squares, rectangles, triangles and also circles. Everyone in Flatland, regardless of their shape, appears as just a line because their vision cannot rise above, nor fall below, the flat surface of the plane of two dimensional existence. The story is about a being from three dimensions, a sphere, who intersects the plane of Flatland.

This simple story gives Abbot ample opportunity to introduce many of the mysteries of higher dimensionality. First of all the sphere, which is a solid object in three dimensional space, crosses through the flat surface of Flatland. When it does, it appears out of nowhere as a dot that becomes a line that increases to some maximum length and then shrinks again to just a dot before it disappears. If you imagine looking edgewise through a sheet of paper, you can imagine that this is how a spherical ball would look as it passed through the paper. The square from the universe of Flatland can only see two dimensions and so it only sees the thin slice of the sphere that intersects its world.

When the sphere passes entirely through Flatland it disappears from the square's point of view. Of course, the sphere can see the square from its position floating above or below the flat surface. From that higher vantage point the sphere can see inside the square's body, which is a shock to the square because even though its insides are perfectly visible from above, they can never be seen from the perspective of anyone else in Flatland. The three dimensional sphere can appear and disappear seemingly randomly in Flatland, but from its point of view it is simply traveling through the three dimensional space of its world.

C. H. Hinton, a British mathematician and friend of Edwin Abott's, made his academic career writing extensively about the fourth dimension. Hinton points out that a cube is a three dimensional object and each of its six faces is a square. That means that the two dimensional squares make up the outer surface of the cube. Similarly the surface of a sphere is also a two dimensional surface although it is curved and not flat. This is why the curved surface of Earth can be traced out, more or less accurately, on a flat map.

By analogy, our three dimensional reality would be the surface of the fourth dimension. What we experience as our solid three dimensional self might be the surface of a four-dimensional being, just like my two dimensional skin is the surface of my three dimensional body. I may be the skin of my four-dimensional self. The world we live in may be just the surface of a four-dimensional world. And all of the space in this universe might be the surface of a four dimensional universe. Now, just like a three dimensional being could appear and disappear anywhere in a two dimensional universe by simply moving through that additional third dimension of space, a four dimensional being could appear and disappear anywhere in our universe.

There are certainly those who understand the mathematics of all this better than I do, but for our purposes the implications are clear without needing to expand on the math. If there is an additional dimension of space then it is right here all around us even though we can't experience it. It is spreading out endless, but in a direction that is inaccessible to us. We cannot experience or even imagine it. Edwin Abott, C. H. Hinton, and P. D. Ouspensky were all obsessed with the implications of the fourth dimension and Ouspensky in particular saw it as the key to understanding cosmic consciousness. For Ouspensky, cosmic consciousness is four-dimensional consciousness and in order for us to experience it we must become our full four-dimensional self.

I want to make sure I don't lose you in all this discussion of the fourth dimension so I want to be clear about a few things before we go on. I believe in higher dimensions of existence, but I don't claim to know what that means. Most simply the thing I feel certain of is that there are vast reaches of reality beyond our ability to perceive or comprehend. I see those as higher dimensions of reality. I am presenting some ideas about a possible fourth dimension of reality because I find it a very helpful exercise. I am not trying to convince you to believe in a fourth dimension, I am offering you a contemplation that I know has the power to stretch your mind. A crucial part of the preparation for cosmic consciousness is stretching your mind, which means expanding your capacity to imagine.

In the end our potential for spiritual transformation is limited by our inability to imagine a different possibility. If we cannot imagine that anything different is possible, it is very unlikely, although you would have to say not impossible, that anything different will ever happen. In my book *The Path of Spiritual Breakthrough* I wrote a great deal about what I call creative illumination. By that, I mean any spiritual practice that is aimed at expanding our ability to imagine new and often paradoxical possibilities. In this form of spiritual work we make the effort to stretch our imagination into inconceivable and unimaginable realms of being. Of course, we will inevitably fail at imagining the unimaginable, and the one thing we can be sure of is that whatever we manage to imagine will at best be a shadow of the invisible reality beyond it. Still, the ultimate purpose of these exercises is not found in the visions they may produce, but rather in the ways they expand our imaginative capacity so that there is space of the miraculous to arise inside us.

The discussion of the fourth dimension is an exercise in creative illumination. I am asking you to make the effort to try to imagine what a four-dimensional reality would be like. You won't be able to, but you will get glimpses. They will be vague, and you will only see them at the periphery of your inner vision. When you turn to see them head on, they will vanish. But you will have glimpses. You will not know what they are glimpses of, but you will be sure that they are glimpses of something different. I said this is a practical book and this is a practical exercise. If you make the effort to stretch your imagination you will create a space inside yourself big enough to hold the vision of cosmic consciousness. Having that space might not be sufficient to ensure the event of awakening, but for most of us it is a necessary prerequisite.

Please don't just read about the fourth dimension here, work to see it for yourself. There may be some things I say about it that don't resonate with you, that is fine just ignore them. As you read, look for ideas or viewpoints where you feel you have some traction. Look for things that you intuitively resonate with or you just feel curious about. Spend time with the things that touch you most and do your best to get inside them and see the view of reality that opens up through them. You won't find something that feels totally satisfying, and it is good that you don't because if you feel comfortable with a vision of the fourth dimension it most assuredly will not be a vision of the fourth dimension.

Ouspensky writes a great deal about the fourth dimension and he talks about the danger of trying to imagine it. He feels that Hinton had fallen into that trap when he tried to envision four-dimensional cubes, and even he himself found it hard to avoid trying to create a mental model of the impossible. The trap that we easily fall into is creating a three-dimensional model of the fourth dimension reality. We can get a better sense of the challenge here by thinking of our own experience of the world. We live in a three-dimensional reality. When I look out at the world I see width, length and height. I am sitting at a table in a café right now. The table top stretches out before me and to my sides, it is also suspended above the floor by its legs. There is a car parked on the street in front of me, a large church across the street, and a fountain in the church yard in front of the church. I see all of that and so much more sprinkled to my left and right, in front and behind me, and at different heights above the ground. I see a three-dimensional world.

I sometimes like to paint pictures and I understand how to paint in perspective. That means I could paint the scene in front of me on a canvas. Anyone who looked at my painting would see that the table was near to me, the car a little further away and to my left, and the church was much further away and considerably taller than both. I would have accurately painted my three-dimensional reality on the two-dimensional medium of the canvas. But, and this is the whole point, the painting is not three-dimensional. I can't reach my hand into it even if it looks like I could. The painting exists on the flat surface of the canvas and the reality of it is limited to that.

To give you another fun example, there are talented street artists who paint holes in concrete sidewalks. The holes look so real that when you notice that you are about to step onto them you tend to jump across to avoid falling in. Safely on the other side you realize that the whole was an illusion painted on a flat side walk, you could have walked right over it.

Whenever we try to imagine four-dimensional reality we will inevitably envision it in three-dimensions. We don't yet have the capacity to perceive in four-dimensions and over and over again we will have a glimpse of a different reality at the outer edge of our imagination, but if we try to see it clearly we will discover that we have created a three-dimensional picture of what we imagine a four-dimensional reality would be. It becomes very frustrating to keep trying as you realize that you just can't imagine the fourth-dimension. Seeing the futility in it, you may be tempted to stop trying. Don't stop. What you are doing with these exercises is pushing yourself up against the limits of your three-dimensional mind. When you push up against the limiting edge of something, you stretch it. Keep stretching. You are expanding your powers of imagination. You are creating room for the dawning of cosmic consciousness. Know that it is worth the effort. You may not see progress, in fact you probably won't, you will see failure, but the work is being done, so don't stop.

Now I want to return to our conversation about cosmic consciousness in relation to the challenge of envisioning the fourth dimension. We could define cosmic consciousness as the direct experience of the all-encompassing oneness of the cosmos. It is the recognition that the cosmos is not a collection of things floating in space. The cosmos is a single living entity that is growing as a whole. In this majestic view we see our own spiritual growth as part of the growth of the entire cosmos. We are the cosmos evolving!

One of the challenges that emerges when we imagine cosmic consciousness in an evolutionary context occurs because our ideas about evolution are wedded to a model of a progressive line of sequential changes. As life evolves, one species leads to the next, one level of consciousness gives way to the next. In this view there is an assumption that evolution occurs along the line of time one step at a time. This is like imagining that your feet evolved into your ankles and your ankles into your knees and then your thighs, your stomach, your neck and then your head. Of course that is not what happened. All of you, from your feet to your head existed from the start and it all grew as part of one unified whole.

If our view of spiritual evolution is wedded to some idea of a sequence of change that happens to things over time, we are not seeing the underlying wholeness of the cosmos. The cosmic evolution that we want to stretch to imagine is one in which everything is growing at once. Time as we know it, doesn't necessarily exist in the fourth dimension. That is why Dr. Ioan Petru Culianu could imagine that the entire history of religion on Earth was being simultaneously created throughout all of time simultaneously by the consciousness of a higher dimensional being as it passed through our three-dimensional space.

Another wonderful way to help stretch your mind is to imagine how the universe expands. Did you know that our universe has no center? The universe that we live in is expanding, but not from some central point outward towards the edges. There are no edges to the universe. The universe is expanding everywhere at the same time. That means that if you go to any place in the universe, you, the entire universe, is expanding from that point outward in all three directions of space. If you move to another point the universe is expanding outward in all directions from there. The same for the next point, and the next and the next. No matter where you go in the universe you will find that the universe is expanding from that point in all directions. How can this be? What is the universe expanding into? Is it expanding into a fourth dimension of space? This is a powerful contemplation. Give yourself some time to think about it and allow yourself to rest against the gentle frustration that arises by not being able to figure it out. That frustration is the feeling of your imagination stretching into the impossible.

I do not want to imply that I don't believe in the current

largely Darwinian theory of evolution, I simply believe that it is a partial understanding. And if we are overly wedded to that linear conception of evolution, then we will almost inevitably see cosmic consciousness as something that will only develop in the future. I mean to show that by embracing the reality of higher dimensions of reality we can begin to discover that we exist in those dimensions already, and the awakening of cosmic consciousness is not a destination that can only be reached in the future. It is an expansion into what is already here beyond our current perceptual limits. You are already a cosmic being and the consciousness of that being already exists within you. The practical guidance of this book is not aimed at becoming someone else, it is about embracing the totality of who you already are.

To further clarify what we mean by cosmic consciousness I want to state that there are two ways that it can be experienced. One is as a direct recognition of the all-encompassing oneness of the cosmos as seen from the vantage point of our three-dimensional self and its three-dimensional consciousness. The other way is the direct recognition that I am the consciousness of the cosmos - the source of universal awareness. In the first case a self-conscious human being recognizes something about the universe. In the second case, the universe awakens to its own existence. This distinction, as we will explore in the next chapter, is recognized in the Hindu tradition as two different levels of awakening. The first we could say is the recognition that *All Is One*, the second is the recognition that *I Am That*.

It is important to remember that the "I" that recognizes that I am that, is not the self-conscious human being, it is the source itself, the cosmos awakening to its own existence. Please play with this difference as it is crucial to our exploration. I suggest that you say the phrase "I am that" out loud to yourself repeatedly. As you repeat the phrase, keep switching who the pronoun "I" refers to in your mind. For a while state the phrase allowing the "I" to be you, the person with your name who is reading this book. After some time, switch so that the pronoun "I" stands for the cosmos itself. Do this exercise switching back and forth every few minutes. Feel the difference between making the statement as yourself and as the cosmos.

Please take the exercise seriously and do it for at least twenty minutes at a time. It may feel like a game to you, like a child pretending to be something it's not. That's ok. Do it anyway. This is another exercise of creative illumination. You are creating space inside yourself for the miracle of cosmic consciousness. As you do the exercise you will notice that when you make the statement as yourself, it feels true. When you make the statement as the cosmos, it feels like pretending. But ask yourself, why? Why does one feel like the real me, and the other feels like pretending? Isn't it only because your identity as the person with your name is more familiar and habitual? There is nothing inherent about feeling yourself to be a person with a name that is more real than recognizing that you are the awareness of the cosmos itself. You have learned to identify yourself as a person who was given your name at birth, but that does not make it your real identity. What if people had told you from birth that you were the cosmos awakening. How would that feel today?

How we identify ourselves determines which form of cosmic consciousness we experience. If we continue to identify as the person who was given our name then we will have a human experience of cosmic consciousness. Inevitably that will be limited by the fact that we will be experiencing the cosmic grandeur in our current form. We will be imagining a four-dimensional reality with a three-dimensional consciousness. This is very powerful and can certainly change your life, but it does not represent the highest potential of the realization.

To experience from the vantagepoint of the cosmos, to realize not only that All Is One, but also to see that I Am That, we have to leave our current identity and allow ourselves to be transformed into a different kind of being. This is why Ouspensky claims that in order to truly experience the fourth dimension we must become four-dimensional ourselves. The difference is seeing the miracle from here vs. stepping into the miracle and being it. The being of it, is what I am referring to as universal being. I believe that this is possible and I believe that it is the possibility that is calling us to our spiritual work. The universe wants to wake up and it needs to do that through us. Our spiritual life was never limited to our personal awakening. We were always being called to participate in the larger awakening of the cosmos itself.

We are essentially speaking here about the difference between spiritual experience and spiritual transformation. We can have a spiritual experience without it leading to transformation. Of course, in the midst of a breakthrough experience we are often swept up into an entirely different state of being. In the moments when the breakthrough is alive within us, we are transformed. Usually we do not remain our normal self having an extraordinary experience. In the midst of the revelation we are only aware of that which is revealing itself to us. Any sense of identity is swept away, at least temporarily. That is a large part of what feels so extraordinary about these moments of higher awareness.

Inevitably the intense peak of the experience begins to fade into memory. Once it is no longer alive in the immediate experience of our psyche it becomes an experience that we had in the past and now only remember having. Habitually we will hold this as a memory not as the truth of who we are. We will tend to think of it as something that happened to us, to our normal self, the one we are familiar with being. Of course, that memory might be held differently. The breakthrough might be seen not as an experience we had, but as an experience of a deeper part of who we are. In this case we recognize that those moments of revelation were not an experience that our normal self experienced, they were a temporary experience of our higher self. The difference between the two is enormously significant. Spend some time working with this idea by contemplating an experience of spiritual breakthrough that you have had. Look at it first as an experience that you remember having, and then look at it as an experience of your higher self. Feel the difference between you having an extraordinary experience and you temporarily becoming your higher self.

What if the experience you had was not just an experience that lit up your nervous system, it was a taste of your true self? What that would mean was that what you saw in that moment didn't come and go. It is not gone now. It is still who you are in a dimension of being you might not currently have access to. The fact that you don't have access to it now, doesn't mean it is not true now. Think of it this way. Turn around and look at whatever is behind your back. Now turn back. What you just saw behind you is not just an experience of something that is now gone. You saw the truth of what is behind you. And even though you are not turned towards it now and therefore can't see it, it is still true. What you saw when you turned around was not an experience that appeared when you saw it and disappeared when you turned back. It is the reality of what is there.

This is how we need to hold our spiritual experiences. We can think of them as glimpses of the higher-dimensional reality of who we are - the energy and intelligence of the living cosmos. We were not just having an experience, we were seeing a deeper truth about ourselves. We are still that. We didn't become a cosmic being when we recognized ourselves as that, we were always a cosmic being and still are. Are you willing to accept the truth of who you are? Are you willing to see the three-dimensional person that you have always known yourself to be, not as the limit of who you are, but as the surface of a much larger being that has always existed in dimensions beyond what your eye can see? I am asking you to stretch into the miraculous right now. This is part of your spiritual work. This is creative illumination. Stretch into the miraculous truth of who you are right now. Embrace your cosmic self, your universal being, your true origin, right now.

There is nothing you need to wait for, no experience that you may have no matter how powerful, will ever make what is true more true. What is true is as true now as it ever will be, embrace it and be done with any doubt about it. You are a cosmic being. You are the universe awakening to its own existence.

Cosmic consciousness is the consciousness of a higher-dimension of being. Our cosmic self is a higher dimensional self. You were always more than what you could see, and you have probably suspected that for a long time. There is no reason to wait to embrace the truth, embrace it now.

I am aware that this idea of embracing a cosmic identity right now may seem far-fetched, maybe even preposterous. Again, I would ask you why. Why does it seem so far-fetched to assume that we are a cosmic being and that our awareness is one with the source of consciousness? It is only because we have been taught to think of ourselves as a separate individual, an isolated organism with a name and an independent source of consciousness. We have been taught to think that way and therefore it seems like the most reasonable way to think. On top of that, everyone else was taught to think the same way so the reasonableness of it is constantly being reinforced in every interaction we have. But the fact that we have been trained to feel this way, doesn't make it accurate. In fact if you think about it a little, it can start to seem preposterous to think that you are an isolated individual with an independent source of consciousness.

First of all, how isolated are you? Can you even live in isolation? Imagine that you are floating in outer space somewhere in the middle of the universe. How long would you last there? Please excuse the gore, but I've heard that if you were out in the vacuum of space without a space suit you would immediately blow up like a balloon to twice your normal size, the water on your eyes and tongue would start to boil off, and you would die within about ninety seconds. So much for being a separate individual.

If you want to live in outer space for any length of time you would at least need to be wearing a pressurized space suit. Your body exists in the atmospheric pressure of Earth, it only holds its shape because it is getting pushed on by the air around it. Your space suit would need to replicate Earth's atmosphere to keep you from blowing up. Then you would need to have air to breathe so your suit would need to carry some amount of compressed air. I've read that space suits can hold about a thirty-two hour supply of oxygen. If we want to live longer than that we need a spaceship that can hold more oxygen and also some water and food. If we want to live for very long periods of time we would need to be onboard a space ship big enough to grow food in.

What you see is that if you want to live in outer space you need to recreate the conditions of planet Earth. That's because we are not a separate thing that just happens to live on the surface of Earth, we are part of Earth. We are inseparable from Earth. I like to say that we exist on Earth the way an air bubble exists in water. The air bubble does not exist separate from the water. You cannot reach your hand into a bucket and scoop out an air bubble. The existence of the bubble is defined by the water. Without the water there is no bubble. In the same way that without Earth we cannot exist either. We are part of Earth.

I like to think of human beings as organs of Earth, like your eyes are organs of your body. We don't think that our eyes see. They are seeing organs, but we are the ones that see. In the same way, it appears to me that we are organs of the consciousness of Earth. We are not conscious, Earth is conscious. We do not exist separate from Earth, we are part of it, so our consciousness is part of it also. This actually makes more sense to me than the idea that I am somehow a generator of a consciousness that is independent from anything else.

The shift into cosmic consciousness that we are exploring is more than a vision of universal oneness. It is a remembering of who we really are. We are a cosmic being, and when we wake up to our true self in this way, it is not the separate human self that is waking up. The universe is waking up through our human form. The shift in identity from a human being to a cosmic being is beyond what we can imagine. It requires us to open to an infinite source. This is exactly the kind of opening that great mystics and spiritual realizers have spoken about for thousands of years. Their descriptions of awakening sound like experiences of opening to a higher dimension of being and an infinite self along the lines of what we have been exploring here.

In the last chapter we looked at cosmic consciousness in an evolutionary context and saw that it was the next step in the evolution of consciousness. It will be as far removed from our present state of self-consciousness, as simple consciousness is from where we stand now. This realization is so valuable because it dramatically expands our sense of scale. It creates a sense of the vast shift that we are pursuing, and it helps us see our own spiritual growth as part of a universal process.

That said, it also has shortcomings, which we have already mentioned. One being that it can be misleading to think in terms of a line of causality. Maybe self-consciousness didn't evolve out of simple consciousness. Maybe they were always co-evolving. After all we are not just self-consciousness, simple consciousness is very active in many of our living functions. Perhaps also cosmic consciousness has always been a part of consciousness even if we did not have access to it.

Ouspensky points out that one of the problems with an evolutionary view of cosmic consciousness is that it tends to push the idea off into the future. If cosmic consciousness is such a dramatic developmental leap from where we are, it seems obvious that it will take a long time and require a great deal of effort. And if our evolutionary view assumes the inevitability of the shift then it can lead to complacency about our own development. If cosmic consciousness is an inevitable growth, like becoming an adult is inevitable for a child, then we don't need to worry about it because it is coming regardless of what we do. But maybe cosmic consciousness is not an inevitable and natural developmental step that must occur after self-consciousness. It seems, at least to Ouspensky, that our current state of consciousness can just as easily impede or stop the process of growth as it can accelerate it. Rather than thinking about the inevitable fate of humanity over an evolutionary time frame, he wants us to think about our personal fate in this lifetime. What matters is not whether or not humanity as a whole is destined for cosmic consciousness, what matters is whether we are going to attain that infinite state of being ourselves now.

Edward Carpenter was inspired by the poetry of Walt Whitman, but also by the writings in the *Bhagavad Gita* and his six week apprenticeship in the Eastern esoteric tradition. Out of the four chapters that Carpenter wrote about his discovery of cosmic consciousness in Ceylon, one of them was devoted to describing the methods of attaining that state. He was profoundly inspired by what he learned from the swami and he was confident that there existed practices that could reliably open the door to higher awareness. Richard Maurice Bucke was a psychologist and a scientist. He saw cosmic consciousness as a natural and inevitable part of the evolutionary development of the cosmos. There is no mention in his book on cosmic consciousness of practices that can lead to it, or even statements of the need for them.

Ouspensky was a mystic and a practitioner. He believed in the power of self-directed spiritual growth. He devoted his life to Gurdjieff because he loved his system for teaching spiritual growth and he would guide students in that system for his entire life, long after he had left the fold and gone out on his own. For Ouspensky, cosmic consciousness is four-dimensional consciousness. We cannot experience it with our three-dimensional awareness. We must expand ourselves into four dimensions, which will take effort.

I want to be clear, how much effort this requires, if any at all, is different for every individual. One of the things Carpenter discovered in his studies in the East is that general rules for spiritual attainment are seldom given because every individual's needs are unique. That is why in the East deep spiritual work is traditionally done with the guidance of a teacher. I don't know what it will take for you to attain this miraculous state. I am sharing with you some of the perspectives, ideas and practices that have been most essential for me. They may also be for you, but you will have to work with them for yourself and adjust and attune them to your specific needs.

I am offering the context of the fourth dimension because it makes clear that even though the shift to cosmic consciousness is huge, and the distance between that state and our present one is vast, the possibility always and only exists right here and now. Ouspensky makes the provocative point that a surface is always the place where two things connect. The surface of an air bubble is where the water connects with the pocket of air. My skin is where my body connects with the world outside. The surface of something will always contain one dimension less than the surface is. The surface of a three-dimensional cube is made up of six two-dimensional squares. The surface of Earth is a two-dimensional surface that can be mapped on a flat piece of paper.

Our entire three-dimensional reality is the surface of a four-dimensional reality that extends infinitely in directions that are completely invisible to us. The critical insight for us to realize is that even though we cannot see the fourth dimension, we are always in indirect contact with it. We and everything around us are its surface, it is always right here just beyond the reality that we can see. We don't need to wait until tomorrow to find it, we don't need to wait for evolutionary epochs to pass before it will be here. It is here now. All we need to do is stretch beyond our current limits of perception so that we can see more of what is already here. When you are lifted up into the being of cosmic consciousness it will feel like home. It will feel like something you have always known. You are already a four-dimensional cosmic being, you just need to learn how to perceive your full self. In the next chapter we will explore the path and practice of cosmic consciousness. We will follow the lead of Edward Carpenter and explore the enlightened vision of the Hindu teachings of Advaita Vedanta. We will embrace a perspective that we can call cosmic nonduality and explore the power of what I will call cosmic prayer.

Before we move on, please take a moment to contemplate yourself as the surface of the fourth dimension. You, your three dimensional self, and the three dimensional world all around you is the surface of the fourth dimension. Take a moment to look around now. Look at everything you see. Imagine that just beyond it all there is a universe that extends in directions beyond your ability to imagine. Keep looking. Keep feeling the nearness of the fourth dimension. If you are thinking of the world around you as if it were like a skin covering another universe, you are thinking in three dimensions. The world you see is not like a blanket covering a sofa. The fourth dimension doesn't exist on the other side of the world in any way that you can imagine. It exists on the inside of everything you see. Not inside in the way that seeds exist inside apples. Inside in a dimension that you can't possibly imagine. Everything has an infinite universe inside of it. I think William Blake expressed it beautifully in these famous lines.

> *To see a World in a Grain of Sand*
> *And a Heaven in a Wild Flower,*
> *Hold Infinity in the palm of your hand*
> *And Eternity in an hour.*

Feel into that.

Now do a second exercise. Look at the world around you.

See how it exists out there away from you. Now look at your skin and imagine the inside of your body. All of your organs and blood vessels are safely enclosed within the surface of your skin. The inside of your body is an inside, but it is still within the visible part of the three-dimensional world, in other words it is still part of the outside world. If you cut your body open you would see that everything in it is there waiting for you to see.

Now look inside your mind. Close your eyes if you need to. Notice the thoughts and feelings and sensations that you free. Where are they located? They are not inside your body. They are not even inside your brain. You can cut open your brain and you will never find a feeling or thought in there. Think about your dreams. You can dream of a mountain and a lake, but where do they exist? If someone sees you asleep they are not going to see any part of your dream. Your dreams, thoughts and feelings all exist in your mind, but where does your mind exist?

Is it possible that your mind is a portal to another dimension? Is it possible that we can change how we think and feel to escape from the perceptual limitations of three dimensions and enter higher dimensions of being. I believe that it is. I believe we can use our minds to enter the full dimensionality of our being, but we can't do it with our habitual ways of thinking and feeling. Instead we need to think and feel in new ways. Creating a bridge to the fourth dimension by developing new ways of thinking and feeling was P. D. Ouspensky's life's work.

In his later years, Ouspensky expressed great dissatisfaction that he had never attained the heights of consciousness he wanted so desperately to realize, but during the last days of his life the students who were attending to him on his deathbed all felt that something had happened. At some point Ouspensky seemed to shift into a different state of consciousness. He communicated with them largely telepathically at that point and the amount of information they received from him was sometimes so overwhelming that they would ask him to stop transmitting. Those who were with him in those days were certain that he had finally attained the cosmic consciousness that he had dedicated his life to.

SUMMARY OF EXERCISES

1. Say the phrase "I am that" out loud to yourself repeatedly. As you repeat the phrase, keep switching who the pronoun "I" refers to in your mind. For a while state the phrase allowing the "I" to be you, the person with your name who is reading this book. After some time, switch so that the pronoun "I" stands for the cosmos itself. Do this exercise switching back and forth every few minutes. Feel the difference between making the statement as yourself and as the cosmos.

2. Contemplate an experience of spiritual breakthrough that you've had. Look at it first as an experience that you remember having in the ordinary sense. Then look at it as if it were a memory of your higher self. Feel the difference between you having an extraordinary experience and you being your higher self.

3. Contemplate yourself as the surface of the fourth dimension. You, your three dimensional self, and the three dimensional world all around you is the surface of the fourth dimension. Take a moment to look around now. Look at everything you see. Imagine that just beyond it all there is a universe that extends in directions beyond your ability to imagine.

Describe in a notebook or journal about what you see in this investigation.

CHAPTER EIGHT

Essentials of Spiritual Attunement

"The spiritual life of individuals has to be extended both vertically to God and horizontally to other souls..."

~ Evelyn Underhill

EDWARD CARPENTER AND MAURICE BUCKE both received a transmission of cosmic consciousness from Walt Whitman's poetry. Bucke claims that his was only a brief glimpse, but changed his life. For Carpenter years of seeking led to a fruition of the experience in Ceylon with a spiritual master. P. D. Ouspensky's life was completely dedicated to the attainment of fourth dimensional awareness, which is how he spoke about cosmic consciousness. He had many powerful spiritual experiences during his lifetime, both before, during and after his time with Gurdjieff, but his efforts by his own accounts did not yield the fruit he sought, until, according to his attendees, he finally slipped into that miraculous state of cosmic consciousness on his deathbed.

The question I want to explore in this chapter is how? How can we successfully invite the miracle of cosmic consciousness into our being? My interest in spiritual life was always similar to Ouspensky's. I wanted to know how to attain enlightenment in this lifetime. I didn't want to learn about the miracle of higher consciousness, I wanted to experience it and live it. I single pointedly dedicated my life to spiritual pursuit. I left my wife and career to join a spiritual community where I could do intense amounts of practice. I have already qualified that the community I was in, and the teacher I worked with, were far from perfect. In fact, many aspects of what was going on were crazy, but still I experienced miraculous openings that were life-changing. In *The Path of Spiritual Breakthrough* I described a number of those breakthroughs and how they altered my perception.

One of those was the experience of comic consciousness and the subsequent memories of that experience in my early childhood that I have already described in this book.

While doing the research for *The Path of Spiritual Breakthrough*, I dusted off my copy of Richard Maurice Bucke's book, *Cosmic Consciousness* and fell in love with his description of the miraculous state all over again. I republished Bucke's book with my own annotations just before I published *The Path of Spiritual Breakthrough*. Something happened to me during that research. It was as if I was experiencing the transmission from Bucke's book for the first time. My excitement brought me to read more of Edward Carpenter and also the spiritual writings of Sri Aurobindo. I slowly began to see my entire life through the lens of cosmic consciousness as I never had before. I realized that this particular manifestation of awakening was the one I had been born for. I came into this life with some memory of my previous cosmic state and that memory drove my spiritual life, initially from the depths of unconsciousness and later as my conscious goal. My desire for the miraculous realization compelled me to constantly question life, to read spiritual books incessantly, to learn and practice meditation, and eventually to step out of my life and join a spiritual community.

As I read Bucke, Carpenter and Aurobindo, I felt that I was being called again. I was being called home. I love my life. I teach meditation and mystical philosophy to wonderful people all over the world. I continue to feel the presence of divinity closely all around me and I still have powerful spiritual openings and breakthroughs regularly. And even with all that, I started to feel called. It felt like an invitation to a new level or dimension of spiritual life was being offered to me. This book was born out of my own personal contemplations about what life I was being invited into. How should I live so that I could spend more time in the state of universal being?

I feel called to explore all of my past experiences, those that were miraculous, those that were awful and everything in between. My initial professional training was as a scientist and the experimental spirit remains central to who I am. The experimental method is the most important thing that I learned as a scientist. No knowledge is ever final, it is always the best you know so far. Science works well when we constantly test our current state of understanding against new ideas and new hypotheses. The other thing that I learned, and this was probably the most valuable thing of all, is that experiments never fail, they just end, and when they do we look at the results, collect the data, and design a better experiment. That is how I felt when my first spiritual community failed. Yes, that experiment had been a very mixed experience, but it had not failed, it had just ended and there was a wealth of data to collect and learn from before initiating a better experiment.

In my writing and when I teach I always want to share the very best I have to give, and right now that means boiling down what I have learned about how to live a life that is optimally attuned to the miracle of cosmic consciousness. I said already that an author always writes in part for his or her own benefit. This book has been even more for my benefit than any of my others because it was born out of a calling I felt toward the next step in my own evolution and a need to be clear with myself about what I was being called to and how I could best answer the call. In this chapter I am going to outline what I see as the essential elements of a life that is optimally attuned to the miraculous. I am outlining the life that I feel is calling me to live it, so I feel the guidelines I am about to write are as much for myself as anyone else. What I am about to write comes from my own lived experience. It represents the fruits of trying, sometimes victoriously and sometimes not, to live a deeply spiritual life. I will not claim to be perfect at living this way, there is plenty of room to improve, but I strive with all my heart to live a life that is guided by all that I am about to share.

To lead us into this conversation I want to speak for a moment about the great hindu tradition of Advaita Vedanta, which was the primary spiritual orientation of my path. Edward Carpenter, as we have seen, was also deeply inspired by this tradition, and P. D. Ouspensky referenced it frequently in his writing as well. Richard Maurice Bucke speaks about cosmic consciousness as Brahmic Splendor, but speaks very little about the path of practice that leads to it. In part to correct for this omission, Dr. M.C. Nanjunda Row, an Indian disciple of the famous Swami Vivekananda, published a book called *Cosmic Consciousness or the Vedic Idea of Realization or Mukti: In the Light of Modern Psychology*. In his book Dr. Row addresses some of the same considerations that Ouspensky would publish about in *Tertium Organum* when he would publish that book a few years later.

The first thing to be said about Dr. Row's book is that he is definitely equating cosmic consciousness with the Eastern attainment of enlightenment. I would agree with Dr. Row, at least to a point. The term cosmic consciousness was created by Edward Carpenter to describe what he had experienced as the goal of the Eastern esoteric traditions. He used a term that he felt would be intelligible to Westerners, but he was naming something he had learned about in the East. I believe that cosmic consciousness and the realization of the non-dual oneness of Brahman are equivalent, but as we have already explored at length, I also believe that creating a new name for something does in a sense create a new entity. It gives new access and alters the thing it gives access to. Remember that naming oxygen was not only a passive discovery of something that was already there, it dramatically changed how chemistry was understood and ignited a revolution in science. So I would want to add some qualification and nuance to the equivocation of Brahman consciousness and cosmic consciousness. Still I see how exploring the attainment of cosmic consciousness through the lens of Eastern enlightenment will help us outline a path that we can follow to the miracle.

Dr. Row is largely in agreement with Bucke's description of cosmic consciousness and similarly sees the attainment of it as the entire point of human evolution. He claims that this view can be found in the ancient sacred texts of Hinduism and has been discussed by great masters of that tradition such as Patanjali, Adi Shankara and Ramakrishna. One important distinction that he points out is that he does not see cosmic consciousness as something that will only come in the future, he sees it as a latent potential that exists in all of us right now. This I feel is an essential understanding to embrace as the context for all of our spiritual work. We are not looking for something that is going to happen later, we are unlocking an inner potential that already exists within us. This has a similar effect to seeing cosmic consciousness as an expansion into a higher dimension of being. That higher dimension already exists just beyond what we can see. In fact it is never separate from what we can see. It permeates us and infuses us already, we simply don't recognize it.

The radical immediacy of cosmic consciousness is a key understanding and it is the core insight of Advaita Vedanta. In the tradition of Advaita Vedanta the ultimate goal is the attainment of mukti, or self-realization. That means liberating your consciousness from the limitation of seeing yourself only as an isolated separate being and realizing your nature as an infinite cosmic being. The orientation that we must adopt to this work is that we are already a cosmic being. The awareness that I have writing this, and the awareness that you are using to read it, are not separate. We are both experiencing the same universal source of awareness. Thinking for a moment about me looking at a mountain from one side, and you looking at it from the other. Imagine that we mistakenly think we are seeing two different mountains. We are not seeing two mountains, we are having two different experiences of the same mountain. There is an analogous situation with awareness. You experience awareness and I experience awareness and we are taught that one is coming from you and the other from me when in fact they are both coming from the same source. My awareness and yours are not different awarenesses, we are having two experiences of the same awareness.

If we think of cosmic consciousness as an experience or a realization that we hope will happen later, then we don't tend to look for it where it is, right here, right now. When we see cosmic consciousness as a latent inner potential that we already possess, or as a higher dimension that we are already immersed in, we start to feel its existence right here, right now. The key insight of Advaita Vedanta is that it is only our seeking for realization somewhere other than here that keeps us from seeing that it is already ours. When we stop seeking, when we stop looking for realization in the future, we will awaken to the miracle that already exists right here, right now, even when we couldn't see it because we were distracted by looking for it somewhere else. Cosmic consciousness is both a huge leap of consciousness, and closer than close. We must embrace both sides of this equation in our search for the miraculous.

Take a moment to sit in contemplation. Use either the idea that cosmic consciousness is a latent inner potential that you already possess, or the idea that it is a higher dimension of being that always exists just beyond the surface of the reality you know. Either way, contemplate it until you start to feel an enlivening energy building in your experience. When you begin to focus on just how close the miracle is you start to feel more alive. Excitement builds because you begin to feel the miracle right here all around and inside you. Hold this contemplation. Look at the things around you and feel the higher dimensionality that they are the surface of. Look inside yourself and feel the higher potential that is already there waiting to be realized and released. This is a powerful contemplation because it charges the atmosphere of your life with spiritual potential.

Ouspensky, in his critique of Bucke, remarks how in speaking of the inevitability of cosmic consciousness, he neglects the obvious fact that his own experience of cosmic consciousness was precipitated by an evening of reading romantic poetry with like-minded friends. Ouspensky rightly points out that if Bucke had been busy with more mundane activities, the miracle he experienced would probably never have been evoked. Generally speaking, awakening requires a conducive atmosphere to occur within, just like plants require nutrients and sunlight to grow. A tree planted on bad soil will not bear fruit. If we want to experience cosmic consciousness and live more fully from universal being, we must generate, maintain and live inside of an atmosphere that is ripe for the miraculous.

I've repeated many times that I wanted this to be a practical guide to cosmic consciousness. That means that it presents ideas, perspectives and practices that can ignite the experience of cosmic consciousness and allow you to surrender to the reality of who you are and live as a universal being. What I have learned over the years is that for all this to be possible we must live in such a way that we feel the possibility of a miracle always immediately alive around us. We must also be constantly inviting that miracle to occur, and finally be ready to give ourselves to it when it comes. If we are living in a way that includes all of these elements then we will be doing all that can be done. The rest is up to grace, karma, and divinity. To be more explicit about how to live in this way, I will speak about what I see as the essential elements of a spiritually attuned life: clarity, passion, receptivity, service, surrender, and love.

Clarity

One of the essential elements of a spiritually attuned life is clarity. Clarity occurs in the domain of understanding. To embark on this journey you need to acquire an understanding about what you seek, about yourself, and about the journey of awakening. Understanding includes everything that you can learn from books and almost all of what you can get from a spiritual mentor. Everything I have written in this book is offered to help you understand and therefore gain greater clarity. Understanding is the most tangible aspect of the path and it is the equivalent of a road map plus an understanding of how to drive and take care of your car, and an understanding of yourself and your own needs. With clarity on those things, you are ready to embark on the journey, but remember none of those are the journey or the goal. They are all part of the preparation.

Right understanding is essential preparation, but it is not only insufficient, alone it is nothing. If you buy the best maps, maintain the car as it is parked in the street, feed and clothe yourself everyday, but never start driving, then you haven't gone anywhere. The domain of understanding is tricky because it is easy to confuse the map with the territory. Sometimes people learn a great deal about the path without ever journeying on the path very far. They sound like an expert when they speak about it, but they haven't gone anywhere yet. A spiritually sensitive person will feel the lack of authentic experience. Understanding can masquerade as experience, and that is why it has such a dubious reputation among sincere spiritual seekers.

That caveat having been made, right understanding is essential. It is like a runway for the flight. Without a runway the plane cannot take off, but the runway is not part of the flight. You need a runway that is long enough, smooth enough, and straight enough to take off from. The direction your runway is pointing toward is important too. If your runway is pointing in the right direction you won't have to turn and course-correct dramatically in midair. I want to share with you a few things about which you absolutely need to have clarity for this journey.

One crucial clarity that we must strive for relates to our intention. You need to know what you want, and you need to know how much you want it. We have already spoken about the fact that if you are reading this book you are undoubtedly already being called to the miracle of cosmic consciousness. Something you saw in the potential of this book spoke to you, and I believe that could only be your previous connection with the state of consciousness that the book is about. In my opinion, the fact that you are being called is beyond question, what is in question is how and to what degree you want to respond. My former teacher insisted that you want to go all the way. In the context that we are exploring that means all the way to a totally surrendered life of universal being. I would agree that if that is the life you want to live, then you have to be willing to give up everything for it, but that is not the only way to live a spiritual life.

I believe that we all have a unique spiritual destiny that plays a part in the symphony of universal awakening. Maybe it is your destiny to live as a fully realized luminous being, but it seems that destiny is rare. Many more people seem to populate the expanse of consciousness between initiation and total realization. In his book *Concerning the Spiritual in Art,* the Russian abstract painter Wassily Kandinsky offered a powerful and simple way to imagine how the awakening of consciousness evolves. He asks us to imagine a triangle. The triangle is full of people and it represents a culture which is traveling upward into new frontiers of consciousness. At the very tip are the most advanced visionaries. There is hardly anyone at that height. The few that are there are seeing possibilities that have never been seen before. The power of their vision and their articulation of it in art attracts those that are just below them and draws them upward. Those at that next highest level then communicate their vision of possibility to those just below them. Each next layer of individuals communicates new possibilities to those below and the attractive power of the new possibilities at every level moves the entire triangle of humanity upward.

There must be those who abide at the spearhead and pierce the utterly unknown, but there also must be artists of possibility at each and every layer who communicate what is next to the layer below. As I see it, your calling to cosmic consciousness already places you fairly high up into the tip of the triangle, not necessarily the very tip, but certainly high up. You have to decide or listen for exactly where you are meant to take up residence. What vision of possibility is yours to share. It may not be at the very tip of the triangle. It might be a few layers down. There is newness to be communicated at every layer. We can only hear the call from a layer or two above, so there must be those who are making the call from the narrowest tip all the way to the broad base of the triangle. Part of attaining clarity is knowing where you are meant to be and what you are meant to be sharing.

A related clarity that needs to be cultivated is the discernment of pride. Our spiritual pride might tempt us to see ourselves as someone who should be at the very tip of the triangle. Because we come from a cultural time that thinks in terms of attainment and winning, we will want to be in the first position. That may not be your destiny. You may be supposed to be very near the base reaching large masses of people with a message that can lift them up to the next higher levels. It isn't better or more advanced to be in the tip, and it isn't worse or less advanced to be near the base. This is not a race or a competition. The clarity we need is seeing where we belong by discovering what is our gift to give and knowing who we are meant to give it to. This is not about being the best, it is about fulfilling our own unique destiny.

Humility means accepting your destiny regardless of where it leads you. Humility also means realizing that you don't know how it all works. Perhaps those who are called to communicate new possibilities to the greatest number of people at the base of the triangle are those who were at the very tip in their last life. In this life they are going to use all of their deep attainment from previous incarnations in service of the greatest number of people. We don't know what is really going on or how it all works, and we will never figure it out. What we can know is where precisely we are being called to be in this life and how we can manifest that.

Another clarity crucial to understanding is how to work with paradoxes. There is a paradox that cannot be avoided in this work. It shows up in many different forms as pairs of opposites that are both true. The fundamental cause of the paradox is the existence of the separate sense of self. There is the original source of consciousness, the *big 'S' Self absolute* as it is sometimes called. Out of that infinite universal and singular consciousness the separate, small 's' self was born. This separate self is identified with a particular human organism that was born and will die. We are both of these. Although the identification with the separate self is more habitual and consistent, we also experience cosmic consciousness and recognize ourselves to be a singular universal being. The *small self* has a view of the spiritual path, yet the same path from the point of view of the *self absolute* is completely different. We are both and we must embrace the paradox that the two different views create.

One way this paradox reveals itself is in terms of the proximity of attainment. From the separate self point of view the universal view is a tremendous leap, but we are already a cosmic being and so the view that we currently have is the view of the cosmic self. The attainment of cosmic consciousness is both tremendously far from our current view, and already inherent in the view we have now. It is a million miles away, and already right here. There is no way to resolve the paradox, it simply needs to be embraced. Our nature includes both the particular and the universal.

Another way this paradox shows up is in the question of effort. From the point of view of the separate self the journey will be long and arduous, from the universal perspective there is nowhere to go and nothing to do. Because we are both of these, there is a great deal of work to do, and none at all. Again, there is no way to resolve this. There will be times when a tremendous amount of effort is required, and other times when we must make no effort at all. If we are surrendered to the path we will be willing to make effort when effort is demanded, and to rest when none is required.

We are conditioned to find it intolerable to live with paradoxes. Instead we crave certainty. For instance there is a part of us that wants to know, *do I need to make effort, or not?* Often there are articulations of spiritual paths that will see only one side of the paradox. There will be those paths that are primarily oriented to working with the separate sense of self. These will be very demanding schools that insist that only hard diligent work over many years, maybe decades, will lead to progress. There are other schools that see predominantly from the universal perspective. These will demand that all effort and all work must be abandoned if there is any chance at all to realize the majesty of who you already are. I believe that both are true because we are both an individual and a universal self. We must embrace all of who we are and learn to discern whether effort or rest is being called for at any given moment. There can be no prescribed path of action, we must learn to listen and respond to what is called for.

As the path to cosmic consciousness unfolds you will continue to gain new understanding. You can recognize the value of new understanding by its energetic quality. Does it bring a sense of opening into possibility? That is the question to ask. If I gain a new insight or understanding and suddenly feel that more is possible I tend to trust it. If a new opening makes a previous one feel constrictive, I let go of the older perspective. Spiritual potential feels like something to me. It is exciting and blissful. It might be intimidating, but not because it is inherently frightening. It is always good, but it can be overwhelming because it is so good. As your path unfolds your clarity will grow and refine. This clarity is crucial preparation for the journey.

Passion

Another essential element of a spirituality attuned life is

passion. The path is fueled by passion. We must be passionate about the miracle of profound awakening. From the point of view of the separate sense of self, this journey will demand a great deal from us, ultimately everything. This perspective is the one that is often emphasized in certain religious traditions, it is certainly the view most forcefully articulated by Dr. Row in his book on cosmic consciousness. In the traditional enlightenment perspective that Dr. Row shares, any attachment to the separate sense of self must be relinquished. The trajectory is from the small self to the big Self. If we are going to successfully leap across the chasm that separates them, we must completely leave behind any foothold on the shore of the small self. Any egotism, any need for personal fulfillment or personal gratification must be abandoned. We must become selfless, the individual sense of "I" must disappear. These schools call for ego death.

This abandonment of the small self is very difficult for the modern seeker to understand and embrace. It has been criticized, and rightfully so, as life-denying, world-hating, and self-destructive. Unfortunately I know from personal experience how true these charges can be in certain ways that this aspect of the path is practiced. In the name of renouncing the small self some schools will encourage and even demand intense hardship and pain as part of the work. Actions that can lead to a negative self image will sometimes be rewarded as spiritually advanced. Taken to extremes this can lead to a loss of identity and experiences of alienation, isolation, and disassociation. None of this holds any spiritual value. It is damaging and if it is forced on someone it is abusive. We will speak later about my belief that our entire spiritual pursuit must be infused with love and that must also include a profound degree of love for our own self.

With all of what I just explained, we need to think about how we can transcend the limitations of our small self-identity without demonizing or damaging it. Having seen or experienced the damaging effects of certain spiritual practices, a person might be tempted to give up altogether. They might decide that they would rather be a happy and healthy individual than a damaged cosmic being. I understand that, and yet I also believe that the path can be embraced intelligently and in a way that allows us to transcend limitations without doing damage. Of course nothing in life is ever risk free, even with the best of effort it seems that few of us manage to be a consistently healthy and happy individual. In spite of the challenge, I do believe that if we embrace the essentials that I am presenting here, we can pursue the ultimate spiritual miracle in a way that is sane and reasonably safe. Of course, I am saying that this journey can be made with reasonable safety, but that does not mean to say that it is not extreme and that it might call for extreme choices.

I believe that the path must always be fueled, driven and guided by your authentic passion for the miracle of awakening. You must always feel that whatever you are doing is what you truly want to do. You should never allow yourself to be pushed or forced into anything. You are on the path because you are passionate about it. You are making extreme choices because you are so authentically committed to the possibility that might result. The goal of the path and the path itself must be your deepest love. You will inevitably love many things in life, but this love must be at least a little bit bigger than whatever comes second. To stay on course you will need to make choices and some of them will be difficult, but if passion is your guide your choices will be yours. Another way to speak about this is in terms of responsibility. We are all responsible for our own journey. We don't want to do anything unless we are willing to be responsible for whatever the result is.

On my journey I was called to leave my first wife to join a spiritual community. I loved my wife and we had a beautiful life together. We planned to have children and raise a family, but when I experienced powerful spiritual openings after meeting my former teacher, I began to feel that I needed to pursue the life that those experiences were calling me to. It was the most challenging decision I have ever made. There was nothing about it that made sense. All I knew was that I had experienced a powerful opening that left me feeling one with everything for a few months and after that I could not stop thinking about it. I was obsessed. I knew that experience was offering me a taste of something that I wanted more than anything else. When it came time to make a decision I considered carefully what I really wanted to do. To my teacher's credit, when I asked him about making such a bold move he told me that we should never take a step bigger than we were ready to accept the consequences for. I thought deeply for a few months and then realized that it was time.

What was interesting about that choice was that the tipping point for me was realizing that if I didn't pursue my dream of a truly spiritual life I would grow resentful. I would never be able to let go of wondering what my life would have been like had I given myself to that opening. I saw clearly that if I stayed I would not be fully behind the plans that my wife and I had made. I actually realized that I already could not go back. The life that I had been living was no longer mine. A new life had replaced it. If I stayed in the life I was in it would not have been good for either me or my wife. If I stayed we would both be compromising the life we really wanted. I saw that she deserved to be with someone who was totally behind the life she wanted to live. It became clear that leaving was the best thing to do. My wife and I had many talks about it. She understood my choice. She actually defended me to our neighbors who all thought I was crazy. I also made sure that I met with both her mother and father to explain in detail what I was doing and why. My wife and I remained on good terms for years, and although I haven't seen her now for over a decade, I am sure we would be happy to see each other if we were to meet today.

That is an example of what I mean when I say that the path can be traveled safely. It has nothing to do with taking the easy road or avoiding hard choices. It has to do with making even hard choices with love and consideration. I believe that it is important for us to consider the impact of our spiritual choices on others and to do what we can to limit the pain our choices create for ourselves and them. Leaving my wife was hard for both of us. I know for a fact that we both spent hours crying over the loss of the love and the life we had enjoyed. The communication between us remained open through the process. I left her materially well taken care of and took very little for myself. I never blamed her for my leaving and made myself available to help her when she needed it. Leaving her was the most difficult and most painful thing I had ever done. I felt the pain of my guilt for leaving her for years, but I also felt that I had done what the divine was asking of me and I had done it as responsibly as I could. As I look back at it today I do not have regrets. That choice was what initiated a new life for me. I feel that I did it as cleanly and compassionately as possible. It created the right stepping off point into the adventure that was to follow.

Another aspect of what we are speaking of has to do with the Eastern law of karma. Karma is both negative and positive. Karma is not about reward and punishment, it is about the way actions grow into the future. If I decide to slap my neighbor, that action will have a life. It will affect the future of our relationship, and might end in a court battle or imprisonment. That is negative karma. I might decide to help an elderly person across the street, perhaps that will lead to them becoming a close friend and me discovering that they are an enlightened sage that I can learn from. That is positive karma. When we do things that come from love and compassion we create positive karma. The things we do might look harsh, we might scold someone, or deny them something they want, but if we are authentically doing it out of love and compassion it will grow into positive effects in the future.

Some spiritual schools hold the miracle of awakening so high up on a pedestal that it seems to supersede any other good. In these schools the ends are thought to justify the means. I believe this way of thinking violates some fundamental spiritual laws and can never ultimately bear fruit. My teacher would sometimes proudly declare that he had no compassion for the ego, only for the true self. At one time I saw this as a sign of his deep spiritual integrity and in some ways it certainly was. Later my understanding expanded to embrace more of the complexity of spiritual life. If the truth is oneness, then the ego and the true self cannot be separate. We cannot love the true self and hate the ego. We must love life in all of its forms and that includes the ego or small self. Love is the only foundation upon which the path can unfold. Love is the beginning and the end. As one who aspires to experience cosmic consciousness and live as a universal being, I believe you must have a deep commitment to be loving and compassionate in all the things that you do, even if they are challenging or even harsh.

Sensitivity

The next essential element that we want to explore is sensitivity. We need to develop a heightened sense of sacred possibility. Some people we meet or circumstances we encounter fill us with a sense of wonder. That person feels like someone who could facilitate your growth, or that circumstance feels like something we could learn from. When a sincere spiritual seeker encounters something like this book, that has the potential to assist them on the path, they feel it. I have done my best to navigate through life based on this sense of sacred possibility. When I feel that energetic opening in my system I follow it. It is like the scent of honey to a bee. It feels sweet and exciting. It promises nourishment. I may not understand why I feel it, but I follow anyway. We navigate the path by following the energy of possibility that opens in front of us. If we follow consistently it will start to feel like a current, as if we were being guided by a river, or following a trail of energetic breadcrumbs that are left on the path. As I have said before, each of us in the end must find our own way home. At the early stage of the path you can use general principles and guidelines to help you, but as you progress your path will become more and more unique. In the later stages you must navigate according to your own spiritual sensitivity and vision.

In direct relation to the subject of this book we must develop our ability to perceive the mystery and higher dimensionality of cosmic consciousness. We have spoken about how that miraculous reality already exists as a latent inner potential or in a dimension just beyond the surface of our three-dimensional reality. You can use whichever metaphor works best for you, but somehow, begin to become sensitive to the immediate presence of cosmic consciousness. Repeat the exercise I offered earlier and feel into that latent potential energy inside you, or outward toward the fourth-dimensional that shimmers beyond and within the world. This is a practice of creative illumination, you need to use your imagination to feel into it. At first it may feel like pretending to you, but as you keep looking and feeling for the cosmic potentials in your awareness, sooner or later you will start finding them.

Another practice that develops spiritual sensitivity is meditation and this practice has been central to my spiritual life since I started on the path over thirty years ago. When I teach meditation I ask people to sit and choose to be content with whatever experience they happen to be having. No matter what occurs, joy or bliss, fear or frustration, find a way to be content with it all. Meditation done this way cultivates spiritual sensitivity by helping you learn to avoid distractions. As you sit and meditate you allow everything to be as it is. Gradually you learn to be quietly content no matter what you are experiencing, whereas before your attention was jumping back and forth between each next thing that arose in consciousness. As you sit for longer periods of time you begin to find yourself moved by a subtle sensitivity. That sensitivity was always there but it could not be felt amidst the louder sensations. As you continue to sit, a world of spiritual energies, visions and insights opens up to you. I have written extensively about meditation in other books, but in relation to this conversation for further instruction the interested reader might want to read my book *How to Be Free: Spiritual Enlightenment, Non-Duality, and Deep Meditation*. I don't believe that the practice of meditation is the only practice that can open up our subtle spiritual sensitivities, but it is a time-honored one. I suggest that you find a spiritual practice that will work for you and do it everyday with your heart and soul.

I also don't want to imply that you should pay attention to these deeper dimensions of spirit only during times of formal practice. The practice of paying attention to the spiritual dimension of reality is something that can and should be done at all times. There is a phrase that describes a person as *in the world but not of it*. When you meet a deeply realized person you often can see that quality in their eyes. They are here but not here at the same time. Their bodies certainly exist in the familiar world all around them, but their eyes have a far off depth to them. They are physically here, but they also seem to see a world of spiritual wonder all around them. If you look at photos of Walt Whitman you can see the deeply awakened inner gaze in his eyes.

I believe we can become more aware of the higher dimensions of reality in the world around us by paying attention and looking for them all the time. Yesterday, I was walking down the street. I allowed myself to relax and let my vision defocus from the familiar world a little. Gradually I found that I was perceiving a subtler dimension of reality all around me. I felt deeper feelings in my being and I saw the shimmering of high potentials everywhere. I passed people on the street and I felt them deeply, but I also felt how we were moving in parallel worlds. I felt both closer to everything and slightly apart from it. Spiritual sensitivities can be developed. You can do this through specific spiritual practices, and you can simply open to them all the time. If you want to experience the miracle of cosmic consciousness, developing your senses in this way is essential.

The last thing I feel it is important to mention about the development of spiritual sensitivity is the role of the body. When speaking about sensitivity it is easy to see this only as a cognitive or emotional sensitivity, but the body is equally essential to our spiritual work. The body is not just a vehicle that holds consciousness, it itself is conscious. Your body is an organ of perception. In order for us to develop the spiritual sensitivity that we need on the path we will need to do spiritual work with the body as well as the mind. My work in the tradition of Ancient Lomi Lomi was a wonderful initiation into the wisdom of the body and that along with the practice of yoga helped me tremendously in developing that embodied sensitivity.

In addition to the wisdom of the body, the journey to cosmic consciousness requires physical well-being. All of the writers that we have heard from in this book agree on this point. A healthy body is essential because cosmic consciousness is not just an idea, it is an energetic transmission, so our bodies need to be ready to receive and hold the higher energies of awakening when they come.

Service

The next element that is essential to spiritual attunement is service. Our spiritual practice and our entire life must be in service of something. When I say this I do not mean in service of an attainment or achievement. I mean on behalf of, or for the sake of, something bigger. Maybe you live a spiritual life for the sake of love, or beauty, or truth, or goodness, or divinity, but whatever you hold as that higher reality that you are living for the sake of, it is not an attainment or an achievement you are working towards. You are living for the sake of the inherent higher qualities of awakening itself. You are living a spiritual life because it is a beautiful life, a true life, a good life, or as Sri Aurobindo called it, a life divine. Our life is purposeful, but it is not a means to an end. We are awakening for the sake of awakening, not as means to achieve or attain something else later. Spiritual life is the end, not because it will bring about something that matters, but because awakening inherently matters. This is why so many spiritual traditions will tell us that the path and the goal are one. We are living a sacred life because it is sacred and not for any other reason.

If we are living a spiritual life in service of the fulfillment of a future goal, even if it is something as beautiful as world peace or universal love, we will not be able to shed the subject/object life of achievement of the separate self. We will still be living in a state that we see as inherently lacking and we will be seeking fulfillment. Our spiritual life ignites with energy and power when we realize that life as it is, even with all of its many ills and evils, is beautiful and perfect as it is. I know this can sound like an avoidance of the obvious facts of existence, but it does not have to. Life when embraced as a whole reveals itself to be a majestic and utterly mysterious explosion of loving goodness. Of course there are many horrible aspects of life, we all see them, but the fact that there is a universe in existence in which imperfection can show up is itself a miracle. The fact that we feel moved to right the wrongs of the world is beautiful. And if we are moved to devote our life to make the world a better and more sacred place that is beautiful. If we are living in service we might be called to serve in many different ways, but we are always rooted in fullness. We are not serving because we need something to change. We are serving because we want to serve. We are fulfilled with life as it is and we are willing to be called into service in any way that our conscience is moved.

For years I worked in social services as a teacher for incarcerated teens. It was difficult work but I was called to make a difference. I was deeply challenged by the overwhelming nature of the problems the teens faced - poverty, racial inequity, lack of education, the breakdown of family structures, and so many others. Over the years I found that the vast majority of the teens would be released from juvenile prison only to become incarcerated adults. There was seemingly no way to stem the tide of imprisonment. I worked in this environment for six years. I was righteously angry about the systems that were failing so many young people. I was always exhausted and on the edge of burn out. One day I became enraged with one of my students and I saw myself clearly. I was angry, not because of what was happening to these children, but because the impossibility of making a difference was stopping me from feeling gratified in my work. I wasn't serving to serve, I was serving to feel good about my life. I was chasing fulfillment. Fundamentally my motives hadn't changed from when I had been an engineer during the five years previous. As an engineer I was seeking fulfillment in material acquisition, when I saw this I changed occupations, but now I saw I was seeking fulfillment through being a helper. That is when I decided to live a spiritual life and dedicate myself to the sacredness of being.

I believe that service of this type is profound. We are not working for any specific end, but in living for awakening we are giving all of our energy to be in service of life. Maybe we will be called to some specific form of service, or maybe our practice and the life that we live will become the service that we offer. When you open to the subtle spiritual intuitions that we spoke about earlier you will start to feel an inherent satisfaction in living a life dedicated to spirit. You will know that you are releasing energy that is benefiting all beings. You will see people all around you and you will know that your life is in some mysterious way helping to create the space for healing, joy, contentment, and satisfaction. You are helping to hold a door of possibility open, a door to divinity, a door to higher dimensions of being, a door to cosmic consciousness. That open door allows the breeze of possibility to enter the world and flow through the world.

Surrender

Everything that I just shared about service must occur within a context of the next essential element which is surrender. Surrender means that we are ready and willing to serve in whatever way we are called. Surrender means giving up control. This is where we can see the underlying truth of why the traditions call us to transcend the ego. It is not because the ego is evil. The ego is beautiful and the formation of it is what made the wondrous leap into self-conscious awareness possible. At the same time, its core orientation of being someone who is living a life for their own sake, prevents us from seeing that we are the source of all of life, inseparably whole and one with everything. As I have said, the ego can have an experience of the wholeness of life, but it can only have it from a place that stands apart from it. The ego can have an experience of "All Is One," but it cannot have an authentic experience of "I Am That!" And by the way, if you meet someone whose ego seems to be declaring *I am that*, I would politely suggest avoiding them.

In order to open to the full majesty of cosmic consciousness we must give up the vantage point of the separate sense of self. That does not mean killing it. The separate sense of self is the critical foundation upon which we must stand. But we must allow the self organizing principle of the ego to operate unconsciously without us focusing our attention on it. We need to forget about it and allow our awareness to be carried to new heights and new vistas. Again think of riding a bicycle, when you first learn to ride you need to pay attention to the activity of riding. The necessity to pay conscious attention to peddling, steering, and keeping your balance, means that your attention is not available to see the magnificent landscape all around you. Similarly, if all of our attention is consumed by our preoccupation with the fears, needs, and desires of the ego, there is no awareness left to enter the miracle of cosmic consciousness.

Offering our spiritual life as an act of service helps release our attention from the grip of the ego. We are relinquishing any sense of personal attainment or future achievement and entering into the sacredness of immediate fulfillment. We are full to the brim with life as it is. We no longer need to seek anything more, even spiritual experiences, because we already have all that we need. We have plenty and so we are free to live in service, not to the attainment of a future goal that we are invested in, but in service of the spiritual life itself. This is the essence of sacred service, and because we have surrendered to that life we are available to be called to serve in any number of ways. We might need to work on behalf of the poor, or the hungry, or towards a healthy ecology, or in any one of so many other ways. There is so much need in the world. We do not have to choose how to serve. It is not up to us. We live in sacred surrender and when we are called to serve we do, happily and gratefully.

Love

The final element that we must speak of is love, and in many ways all of the others can be wrapped up into this one element. A life of spiritual attunement is a life of love that is finely attuned to love. I believe that love is the most stable and powerful foundation for any spiritual work. Your love for awakening, for higher dimensions of possibility, for cosmic consciousness, for divinity, or however else you identify your spiritual passion, must become the light that guides you. The Christian mystic Saint John of the Cross wrote a beautiful poem called *The Dark Night of the Soul*. The poem has been sought for centuries by those needing solace from life's inevitable hardships, but the poem is more generally about how we must navigate through the spiritual path guided by love.

We begin on the path, the poem claims, overwhelmingly aware of the life we are leaving behind. When we steal out into the dark night of the mystery of divinity, we can still clearly see the lights of our old life behind us. For a time we simply walk in the direction of the darkness away from our old ways, but there comes a time when we cannot see our old ways of being in the distance and we cannot yet see the light of the divine up ahead. We are in the middle of the dark night of the soul. The light of divinity is still invisible to us and our old ways are too far behind for us to use them for navigation. At this point we feel lost and forsaken. Our beloved who lured us out into the mystery has left us alone. At this point we might be tempted to turn and return to the life we lived before, or we might be tempted to give up and break down. But there is a third option. At this critical spiritual juncture we must look for the inner light of our love for the divine. If we find that love within us, its light will shine forth and guide our path forward. Our love of the mystery always directs us toward the divine, or to use the language we have adopted in this book, toward great possibility. In the end, as I have said in different ways already, the love that brought us to the path in the first place must become the guide that we trust to take us home.

I don't want to limit the essential love of the path to spiritual love. Our success in navigating the invisible road to higher potentials also depends on loving others. We do not journey alone, we are one of many who are on the path, and we journey amidst many more who have not yet consciously entered onto the path. I believe it is crucial to love all those whose lives we interact with. Our consciousness is not isolated, it is deeply shaped by the people around us. By being in loving relationship with other people, and with our own self, we create a powerful and nurturing relational atmosphere around us. We are always part of a community, whether it is explicit or not. No one is an island, we live and exist together. Your journey to cosmic consciousness will be well served by acting in loving ways with those around you. Your love for the higher potentials of spirit, your love for other people, and your love for yourself, are all absolutely necessary as part of the journey.

In the Hindu tradition there are considered to be two main routes to awakening, jñāna and bhakti. The path of jñāna is the path of wisdom and insight. On this path we strive to see through our exclusive identification with the separate self and discover the universal aspect of being. The path of bhakti is the path of love and devotion. On this path we approach the divine with deep love and reverence. In the end we must work with both wisdom and love, but most of us begin with one or the other first. My teacher taught a path of wisdom and insight, but also encouraged love and devotion. My personality lends itself to a bhakti path. I loved my teacher, I loved my path, I loved the possibility of spiritual freedom. I spent many hours bathed in emotions of deep and intense love that would often bring me to tears. The spiritual path depends on both wisdom and love, but for me and maybe for some of you, love has proven to be the more powerful vehicle for awakening. If we have any fears of the power of love, if we are worried that we will get swept away beyond reason, we must find a way to safely transcend those fears and fully unleash all of the love we hold in our hearts.

We have now explored what I see as the essential elements of the path of cosmic consciousness. These are not the only elements, but they are the most general and those that I feel safe to say will be a part of everyone's path. Of course everyone's path will vary, these elements will be weighted differently for one person than another. And there are many more aspects of the path that will need to be engaged with on the journey forward. You will need to become sensitive enough to discover what your journey needs to include and courageous enough to embrace it.

One final comment before we move on to the last chapter. I don't want to leave you with the impression that these elements, *clarity*, *passion*, *sensitivity*, *service*, *surrender*, and *love*, represent some kind of progression. They are not steps that occur sequentially, and they are not rungs on a ladder that you climb. It would be better to think of them as flavors in a soup. You need all the flavors present to create the right taste of the soup. When all these elements are alive in your life they will work on you. They will open you in ways you cannot imagine. You will steep in them like a tea, and they will reveal the deeper dimensions of your being.

SUMMARY OF EXERCISES

1. Look at the things around you and feel the higher dimensionality that they are the surface of. Look inside yourself and feel the higher potential that is already there waiting to be realized and released. Do you start to feel an energy building inside you?

2. Contemplate each of the essential elements of the path of cosmic consciousness - *clarity*, *passion*, *sensitivity*, *service*, *surrender*, and *love* - and see how they are each represented or not in your own life. If they are not represented, can you think of anyway to add more of this element to your life.

Describe in a notebook or journal about what you see in this investigation.

Chapter Nine

A Life of Cosmic Prayer

"The divine manifests upon earth whenever and wherever it is possible."

~ The Mother

Jeff Carreira

So we have come through our journey and I have shared all I have to share with you about the path of cosmic consciousness. All that remains is to leave you with some concluding thoughts that put everything we have discussed together and to offer some additional inspiration from my own experience that will fuel your own journey.

First of all I want to reiterate my conviction that cosmic consciousness is a real experience of a completely different level of awareness that can become the basis for a completely different way of being. I have no doubt about this and if you want to travel far down this path, you will need to become as certain about it as I am. You might already be, and probably are, but if not please look more deeply into it. Spend time with spiritual people who seem to represent these higher possibilities. See if you feel something different in them. Read books, do practices, follow the guidance that I have offered in this book, pursue this until your own experience tells you that cosmic consciousness is possible and you find that you not only want to experience it; you want to live it.

In 1868 Edward Carpenter read Walt Whitman's *Leaves of Grass* and received a transmission of a new way of being that ignited an inner revelation. In Ceylon, over twenty years later his cosmic prayers were answered and he experienced a completion to his initiating experience. He saw and experienced a miraculous possibility for human life. He called it cosmic consciousness and described it in writing. In articulating his experience he was recasting the traditional Eastern goal of enlightenment for a modern Western audience. Carpenter's friend Richard Maurice Bucke would use Carpenter's phrase as the title for his own book which would eventually attract the attention of William James and through James many others.

Over the next few decades many well known Western and Eastern mystics would comment on Bucke's work and add their insights to it. We have already spoken about how Dr. M.C. Nanjunda Row felt compelled to make the connection to the Eastern conception of mukti clear, and I have mentioned Sri Aurobindo's love for Carpenter's poetry. The notion of cosmic consciousness also caught the attention of the great Christian sage Evelyn Underhill who quotes Edward Carpenter via Bucke in her magnificent book *Mysticism* in which she offers a critique of what she calls the Cosmic Idea. There was also the popular American spiritualist and mentalist Alexander J. McIvor-Tyndall who, writing under the pen name of Ali Nomad, wrote his own extensive treatise called *Cosmic Consciousness: The Man-God Whom We Await* in which he emphasizes the role that sexual energy plays in initiating this higher state. We've spoken at length about P. D. Ouspensky's ideas of the fourth dimension and finally there is also the influential French Jesuit priest Pierre Teilhard de Chardin whose awakening was based on an experience of cosmic consciousness, or a cosmic sense of wholeness, and wrote about it in an essay called *Pantheism and Christianity*.

By the middle of the twentieth century the phrase was firmly implanted in the culture of alternative spirituality. In 1962 Michael Murphy and Dick Price founded Esalen, the famous American spiritual and cultural center that was inspired by the evolutionary spirituality of Sri Aurobindo and The Mother. By the time I was reading *Captain Marvel* in the 1970's I was able to find a fictional teaching of cosmic awareness described as a superpower. By the time I was twenty-nine years old in 1992 I was ready to surrender my life to a teacher who taught what he called evolutionary enlightenment.

Cosmic consciousness as a Western recasting of traditional Eastern enlightenment became an opening in consciousness. A possibility had been born, perhaps not to an entirely new form of awakening, but at the very least a new avenue toward it. The idea of cosmic consciousness as a sense of universal wholeness, an evolutionary expansion and a new dimension of being, captured the imagination of the modern mind in the East and the West. The idea inspired countless spiritually open souls and found its way into both spiritual writing and pop culture. It was a spiritual opening. If we think back to the ideas of Dr. Ioan Petru Culianu, we might see this as a conscious being from a higher dimension that is passing through the three dimensions of our consciousness, or perhaps the division that separates our dimensional reality from the fourth dimension is thinning or maybe the cosmos is waking up. Whatever metaphor we use, it appears that something is happening in the collective mind of our species.

Those of us who are sensitive to this emerging phenomenon feel the opening as a personal awakening, but our awakening is also part of a larger awakening, and perhaps a universal or cosmic awakening. We are, as Arlo Guthrie described to me, catching the wave as it rises up out of the ground, or perhaps passes through from another dimension. This book is a practical guide and throughout I have offered actionable advice and now it is time to offer my last piece of guidance. I want to introduce you to the idea of cosmic prayer.

In the last chapter we explored what I consider to be some of the essential elements of a life of spiritual attunement, by which I mean a life that is optimally attuned to the possibility and reality of cosmic consciousness. I made it clear that the essentials I mentioned are not the only elements that will be needed for your path, but I do feel that they are essential, at least to some degree, on everyone's path. It should also be clear that these essentials do not represent steps to be followed that lead somewhere. We used the metaphor of flavors in a soup to describe how all of the essential elements work and blend together. When you live a life that is permeated throughout with the essential elements of spiritual attunement, your life becomes a cosmic prayer.

A cosmic prayer is not a practice that you do within your life. It is what your life becomes when it is lived for the sake of cosmic consciousness. A life of cosmic prayer acts as an invitation to the miraculous. Imagine a beacon of light on the dark surface of Earth at night that calls out to an alien spacecraft so that it knows a place that is available for a landing. Our life of cosmic prayer is a continuous call, an invitation to divinity allowing her to know that we are available for the miracle of cosmic transformation. I like to personify divinity in female form, so I imagine her as a magnificent higher dimensional cosmically conscious being passing through our three dimensional reality. She wants to pass through, she wants to bless this reality with her higher gifts, but perhaps she can't do it without us. Maybe she can't force her way through our reality, maybe she needs to be invited. She needs the opening that a spiritually attuned life provides. Once she finds a spiritually attuned life, she has the opportunity to flood into this world, and the more attuned and open we are, the more of her high dimensionality is allowed in.

This is how I feel it. I feel her always wanting to find her way into fuller realization here on Earth. I said earlier that I am writing this book because I feel called and invited to a deeper and closer relationship with her. I feel as if my request for cosmic passage has been approved and now it is up to me to travel to that new reality. Writing this book and all of the research, contemplation, and meditation I did to prepare for it, became part of the cosmic prayer of my life. As I experience it, we live the essential elements of a spiritually attuned life, not as a means to an end, not as a way to get what we want, but only because we love the possibility and want to express our devotion to it with our entire being. In living this life we must find a way to embrace the paradox that we are in love with a miracle with all of our heart, while at the same time we are perfectly satisfied to live our cosmic prayer even if it is never answered. It is enough for us to express our love and devotion. Our fulfillment is found in our love for the divine.

When we sit in meditation we are content with just being. No matter what arises in our consciousness, we are content and at peace. We are not meditating so that cosmic consciousness will dawn on us, we are meditating as an act of devotion. Through our complete surrender we are demonstrating perfect faith and trust. We know that she is giving us everything we need right now and we are grateful for all of it. When we study and contemplate higher dimensional ideas we are not doing it to learn and accumulate knowledge. We are not seeking for the secret that will unlock the door to the higher mysteries. We are demonstrating our love through our insatiable curiosity to know her in all the ways that she can be authentically expressed. Our life as a whole is offered to the higher dimensions that exist just beyond the surface of the ordinary world around us.

We do not offer our life as a cosmic prayer as a means to achieving answers or having experiences, but if we are sincere in our offering you can be certain that she will respond. She will give us the insights, experiences and challenges that we need to grow into greater wholeness. She is building her home in us, creating space for the fourth dimension to infuse this world. And our life also becomes complete as a result.

I received a gift of grace while I was researching and preparing to write this book, a visitation from the divine that helped fuel my passion for writing. I was reading numerous books about cosmic consciousness, contemplating what I found, and meditating. Along the way I experienced a breakthrough around the concepts of "involution and evolution" that Sri Aurobindo and The Mother spoke of. I knew that I understood the idea intellectually, but I felt that my grasp was purely intellectual and thin. I wanted to make direct contact with the reality of what this idea pointed to. I became fascinated to the edge of obsession with it. I read about it and thought about it compulsively for a few weeks.

Then one morning I woke up in the middle of a dramatic and visceral revelation. I experienced the totality of my mind and body as part of the Earth. As I woke up and opened my eyes it was clear that my entire manifest being was made of the same "stuff" as the Earth. You could call that "stuff" manifestation or existence, but it was clear that whatever you call it, the Earth was made of that and so was I. Existence itself was the fundamental stuff of reality and everything is created from that. I might appear to be separate from the Earth, but I am no more separate from it than soil, or rocks, or beaches, or rivers. I am part of the Earth.

Simultaneously, it was clear that the awareness that was having this revelation was not coming from the Earth. The awareness was a conscious life-energy that was shining into and through manifestation, into and through the Earth from somewhere beyond it. The awareness that was having the revelation was divine and I saw how the light of divinity penetrates the Earth and stimulates our planet to reach toward the source of the light of awareness. I, in my human form, am an extension of Earth reaching toward the light, and the more light I open to, the more the Earth is compelled to reach through me toward the source. Involution is the light of divinity penetrating the Earth. Evolution is Earth's reflexive reaching back toward the source of the light.

I woke up that morning to the realization that I was that part of the Earth that was reaching toward the light, and I was also the light of divinity shining into the Earth and calling it toward higher dimensions of being. I was involving and evolving. It was stunning. I am still reverberating with the power of the recognition as I write about it now. This experience was the answer to a cosmic prayer that my life had been for weeks.

As I mentioned already this book was born in large part out of my recognition that I was being given the opportunity to enter a new depth of spiritual life. I saw that I was truly born into the possibility of manifesting cosmic consciousness on Earth. I became obsessed with the reality and immediate presence of that higher dimension of being. I saw that my focus on this reality would open up new spiritual worlds for me and would shape and focus the future of my work. I have continued to read numerous books and as I read, I contemplate. I go for long walks and think about what I discover. I use my imagination to explore it. I talk to people about it. It becomes the context for my meditation practice. All of this focus was a cosmic prayer that I offered to the divine. And then one morning she gifted me with a revelatory experience that strengthened my conviction and fueled my passion.

This is how the path of spiritual breakthrough works, and a life of spiritual attunement unfolds. Your focus, contemplation, meditation, and study make your life a prayer. You live in that prayer, steep in it, relish in it, and eventually the divine will answer. When the answer comes it will be a gift of revelation. It will not come in any form you expect. It will not be something you could have imagined beforehand, but you will know that your prayer has been answered. You will feel the higher dimensional reality of the answer. You will feel blessed and grateful to have a part to play in the immense awakening of the cosmos. And with a humble and overflowing heart you will go on living your cosmic prayer for the sake of the higher dimensional reality that it serves.

SUMMARY OF EXERCISES

What contemplation, meditation, and study are you engaged with, what is the cosmic prayer that these efforts are aimed at? Describe in a notebook or journal about what you see in this investigation.

Selected Bibliography

Abott, Edwin. *Flatland: A Romance of Many Dimensions.* Dover Thrift Editions, 1992.

Abrams, David. *The Spell of the Sensuous: Perception and Language in a More-Than-Human World.* Vintage, 1997.

Abrams, David. *Becoming Animal: An Earthly Cosmology.* Vintage, 2011

Aurobindo, Sri. *The Future Poetry.* Lotus Press, 1994.

Bucke, Richard Maurice. *Cosmic Consciousness Annotated: As Edited, Updated and Interpreted by Jeff Carreira.* Emergence Education, 2021.

Carpenter Edward. *From Adam's Peak to Elephanta: Sketches in Ceylon and India.* Wentworth Press, 2016.

Carpenter Edward. *Towards Democracy (Annotated): Poems of Cosmic Consciousness.* Emergence Education, 2022.

Carreira, Jeff. *How to Be Free: Spiritual Enlightenment, Non-Duality, and Deep Meditation.* Emergence Education, 2022.

Carreira, Jeff. *The Path of Spiritual Breakthrough: From Awakening to Cosmic Awareness.* Emergence Education, 2021.

Dewey, John. *Human Nature and Conduct.* Dover Publications, 2012.

Hinton, Charles Howard. *The Fourth Dimension.* Otbebookpublishing, 2022.

James, William. *The Varieties of Religious Experience: A Study in Human Nature.* Routledge, 2008.

Kandinsky, Wassily. *Concerning the Spiritual in Art.* Translated by M. T. H. Sadler,Dover Publications, 1977.

Kripal, Jeffrey J. *Authors of the Impossible: The Paranormal and Sacred.* University of Chicago Press, 2011.

Kripal, Jeffrey J. *Mutants & Mystics: Science Fiction, Superhero Comics, and theParanormal.* University of Chicago Press, 2011.

Kuhn, Thomas S. *The Structure of Scientific Revolutions.* Enlarged 2nd ed.,University of Chicago Press, 1990.

Ouspensky, P. D. *Tertium Organum: A Key to the Enigmas of the World.* Delhi Open Press, 2021.

Row, Dr. M.C. Nanjunda. *Cosmic Consciousness or the Vedic Idea of Realization or Mukti: In the Light of Modern Psychology.* G. A. NATESAN & CO., 1909.

Starlin, Jim. *"Metamorphosis." Captain Marvel The Complete Collection,* Marvel Comics Group, 2016.

Whitman, Walt. *Leaves of Grass.* Oxford University Press, 2005.

About the Author

Jeff Carreira is a meditation teacher, mystical philosopher and author who works with a growing number of people throughout the world. As a teacher, he offers retreats and courses guiding individuals in a form of meditation he refers to as *The Art of Conscious Contentment*. Through this simple and effective technique, he has led thousands of people in a journey beyond the confines of fear and self-concern into the expansive liberated awareness that is our true home.

As a philosopher, Jeff is interested in defining a new way of being in the world that will move us from our current paradigm of separation and isolation into an emerging paradigm of unity and wholeness. In his books and lectures, he explores revolutionary ideas in the domains of spirituality, consciousness, and human development. He creates courses and programs that encourage people to question their most foundational experience of reality until previously held assumptions fall away leaving space for a dramatically new understanding to emerge.

Jeff is passionate about the potential ideas have to shape how we perceive reality and how we live together. His enthusiasm for learning is infectious, and he has taught at colleges and universities throughout the world.

Jeff is the author of numerous books including *American Awakening*, *Philosophy Is Not a Luxury*, *The Soul of a New Self*, *Paradigm Shifting*, and *The Art of Conscious Contentment*.

For more information visit: jeffcarreira.com or scan the QR code below.

Made in United States
North Haven, CT
22 October 2023

43044948R10107